MAKING LOVE

TOM INGLIS

MAKING LOVE
First published 2012 by
New Island
2 Brookside
Dundrum Road
Dublin 14
www.newisland.ie

P/B ISBN 978-1- 8484-0130-3
ePub ISBN 978-1- 8484-0136-5
emobi ISBN 978-1- 8484-0137-2

British Library Cataloguing Data. A CIP catalogue record for this book is available from the British Library.

Typeset by Mariel Deegan.
Printed by ScandBook AB

New Island received financial assistance from
The Arts Council (An Comhairle Ealaíon), Dublin, Ireland.

10 9 8 7 6 5 4 3 2 1

MAKING LOVE

Arron and Olwen

1

Aileen lay dying in bed beside me. I looked out through the window. There was still life outside. The landscape of the rooftops on Winton Avenue was as it always has been. The weather and seasons brought changes, but there was the same vista of houses and gardens. She would go, but they would go on: sucking in life and death.

Inside our house, in our bed, all that was solid and beautiful was melting into air. I was a frightened rabbit staring into the headlights of the car that was about to run me down. The meaning that we had created over so many years was evaporating.

It was approaching the end of May, thc nicest week in the nicest month of the year. The morning sun glistened on the roof slates. The trees were in leaf. The birds were in song. The sounds of the children playing in the school yard at the end of Winton Avenue drifted in through the open window.

She was asleep on her side. I lay behind her, listening to the rhythm of her breathing, staring out the window. It was laboured and erratic. She would go from long, troubled breaths to being completely still. There was a titanic struggle going on within her, between life and death. Death had the upper hand, but she was fighting hard.

As each breath came, I wondered if it would be her last. Sometimes the gap between the breaths was so long, I was convinced that she had died. I lay there motionless. I was beyond thought. I was just feeling. Was this it? Was it all over? And then I would feel her body move. We were off again, into another breath, into more life. She was back from the brink.

It was as if I had been cast as an unwilling actor in a weird play. It was unfair. I was used to making love. Here I was making death. What do I do? What words and moves do I make? I had no idea what to do. I was making it up as I went along. Yes, I had some experience of death. I had been with Mum when she died, but she was of an age to die. This was different. This was so intense. Life and death were merging into one.

I wanted to go to the bathroom, but I was afraid she might die while I was gone. I started twitching nervously, holding myself in. I couldn't leave until she wakened, but I couldn't hold on any longer. I slid out of the bed, out of the bedroom, up the short flight of stairs into the bathroom. Letting go my pee helped me relax, so I took time to wash my teeth and shave. It made the morning seem normal.

When I came back down to the bedroom she was awake. She was in a cold sweat with a pale, horrified look on her face. I got back into bed beside her. I held her. I tried to comfort and reassure her. She was a young girl again, terribly frightened by something. She told me in a halting, sobbing voice that she had had a nightmare. She had been in this blue light, and she tried to waken from it but couldn't. In the dream, she let go. She dreamt that she had died. But then she woke up.

If you stare for long enough out our bedroom window, concentrating on the far distance, to the horizon where the houses meet the sky, you eventually see nothing. There is a sense of transcendence, something in between meaning and meaninglessness. How often did she stare out the window, wondering what it was going to be like to die?

Even before she became ill, Aileen spent hours looking out the bedroom window. It was a slow, pensive, untroubled look. Often I would be sitting in my chair beside the bed, reading. I would glance over at her and look at her looking out over the skyline, away with her thoughts. In those final days and weeks, she seemed to be looking out the window more often.

I have no idea what she was thinking. I suspect she was looking back. She certainly wasn't looking forward to death. She loved life too much. She was still living in hope. Even in that last week, she talked animatedly about the things that we would do together. It was as if she could talk herself out of death.

She calmed down from her nightmare. I talked about bringing the dog for a walk, getting the newspaper, bringing up breakfast. In this weird play of life and death, I could act as if it was any other morning. I wanted to be ironic, to make a joke of it all, to look death in the face and laugh. But I said nothing. Dying is no joke. She moved from her nightmare about dying to trying to stay alive.

'Tom, remember I have to go in to do my bloods today.'

She had an appointment in the hospital. It was all madness: how was I going to get her down the stairs, into the car, drive over to St Vincent's and get her out of the car and into the hospital? She was unable to walk. She was a dead weight. What if she fell as we made our way down the stairs?

And what would the blood tests reveal? Everyone knew she was dying. Kay, the hospice nurse, had told me two days previously that it would only be a matter of days. Kay was an expert in death; watching, monitoring, caring for the dying. How many people like Aileen had she brought to the brink of life and helped over to the other side? Kay was able to read all the vital signs. She was a kind of 'mid-mother' bringing scared adults to death. She did not need test results to tell her how close Aileen was to dying.

Aileen had become addicted to going for tests and getting results. She had kept a meticulous record of every test she had done since the cancer came. She had notebooks, folders and files. She entered the results for all her tests. She recorded all her treatments and the drugs she took. She kept a diary of her diet, trying to link her feelings of well-being with what she ate and drank. She devised a graph which measured the level of pain from one to ten. Each day she entered a recording. She had a monthly review of her pain chart in light of her drugs, treatments and diet. Blood test results were central to her record keeping. If there were no blood tests, there would be no results. There would be nothing to enter in her charts. The file would be closed.

It was all a grand delusion. She was looking desperately for signs that she was not dying. She hoped for a dramatic change that had happened deep down in her body, a startling fight back by the anti-cancer forces, which neither she nor Kay could see. Maybe she was feeling better, maybe she was making a dramatic recovery, maybe a miracle was taking place, maybe she was not going to die after all.

I was being cajoled into the make believe. It was time to tell the truth, to say what had been hinted at before: this was the end of the road. There was no hope, no light at the end of the tunnel. This was death, the end of a beautiful life. But how could I avoid bursting her bubble of hope? How could I let the air out of her life gently?

'Tom, I have to get dressed. I have to go the hospital.'

It was decision time. I had to be patient. I described the difficulties, the pain and discomfort of getting her into and back from the hospital. She was silent. She was not happy. She did not like that I was making the call on this. I suggested that I would phone the hospital, describe her circumstances and ask their advice. The reality was that the hospital people were removed from the scene. Her appointment had been made a month ago. They had no idea how much she had deteriorated, particularly in the last week.

When I phoned and explained, they said there was no need for her to come in. They suggested that I ask her doctor, my cousin Olivia, to come to the house, collect the bloods, and bring them into the hospital. It was all madness, looking for signs of health and illness in someone queuing up to die. And so the delusion continued.

Olivia arrived. For half an hour she searched up and down Aileen's hands and arms trying in vain to find a vein that she could use to extract the blood. Olivia too knew that the game was up, but she was forced to play on. She told Aileen, quietly and calmly, that even if she did find a vein, and even if she did manage to get the needle in, it would be unlikely that she would be able to extract enough blood.

Aileen sighed. It was a sigh of acceptance. The sigh a child gives when she finally realises that, despite all her pleading and protests, she is not going to be allowed go out, watch more television, have one last biscuit. It seemed as if the play was over but Olivia threw her a lifeline, a thin thread of hope. Maybe, she told her, she might come back later and try again. But Aileen had given her sigh, she could see that it was pointless. It was a generous offer that was not meant to be accepted.

After Olivia left, there was silence for a while. The enormity of what was happening began to sink in. The ship was sinking, and so all that previously could not be said, was said.

'Tom, this is all happening very quickly isn't it?'

'Yes, my love.'

'Will you lie down beside me?'

And so for some time we lay together. I was crying. I did not want to, but I could not help it. As we lay and held each other and looked out the window, we talked. We had lain like this many times before in those ethereal moments after making love. Lying, holding, talking, drifting in and out of sleep, searching lazily for words to keep our thoughts going, waiting to see if our passion had been fully extinguished.

'Tom, can we make love?'

I cried. How could she think of making love now, just moments after she had accepted she was dying? Was this Aileen at her most bizarre? Or was it her at her most beautiful? To have the desire and determination to defy death by making love. Maybe she felt that the best way to embrace death was to embrace life, to relive the ecstasy of thousands of times before, to savour for the last time the world of love beyond words, the intense pleasure of physical intimacy.

She became calm and serene. The anxiety and stress began to dissipate. There was a glow to her face, the return of her smile, and lightness to her being. Making love had been a good tonic for death.

But she was still determined to fight to the last. She would do everything that could be done to squeeze whatever more time and pleasure she could get from life. She phoned the hospital and got through to her oncologist. She asked him straight how long he thought she had. He said a month, maybe more. Another line of hope, but I suspect that she knew he was playing her along.

That night, having washed her and helped her take her morphine pills, I collapsed into bed. I was exhausted. We were lying silently for many minutes. I wondered what she was thinking, what petty hopes and desires she had, what were her last wishes. I was hoping for sleep to come quickly and easily. I began to drift off, then heard her voice, strong and determined:

'Tom, I haven't brushed my teeth.'

'Could we please leave it, my love? I am really tired.'

'Tom, you know how crucial good dental care is when you have cancer.'

I screamed silently. I went up to the bathroom, brought down the toothpaste and brush, and patiently brushed her teeth.

The next day, she was a new woman. There was not a whiff of delusion. She accepted she was beaten. She began to let go. I began to tempt her with food pleasures that she had always enjoyed but, as part of her strict diet, she had denied herself: bacon and scrambled egg, a toasted cheese sandwich, creamy mashed potato.

She sat silently, staring into space, but her face lifted, her eyes widened, she began to smile. She was like a child who, having been told so often that she could never eat sweets again, was being led into a sweetshop and shown all the lovely chocolates, biscuits and bars she could have. She was mesmerised by all the choice. She wallowed in the imagination of the different tastes and flavours. But it was all an impossible dream. The reality was that because her liver had become so swollen with tumours, it had pushed her oesophagus so far over that she could barely swallow her tiny pills of morphine.

I had to be inventive. She could not swallow, and her mouth was drying up from all the morphine. I tempted her with some homemade ice-lolly pops. The distraction seemed to work. She lit up with excitement, and we explored the possible flavours: orange, pineapple, pear, maybe even strawberry? She became giddy with anticipated delight. The irony was that there was never any prohibition against ice-lollies; she could have had oodles of them all through her dietary regimes.

I wanted her to have something sumptuous and exotic, maybe seafood and champagne. It would have to be something that would not be destroyed by being liquidised. Something that she could sip or be spoon fed. We were thinking and talking when she leaned over and took my hand.

'Tom, I know it. I would love some chicken soup.'

I danced down to the kitchen. Maybe in the middle of dying we could have a little celebration? It was difficult for those in the kitchen to read my excitement. Our daughter Olwen, son Arron and his girlfriend Jenni were there with Aileen's sisters, Carol, Trish and Maura. They all seemed to freeze in mid movement as I came in. What had happened? Had there been a turn for the better, a little miracle?

When I mentioned the chicken soup, the silence erupted into a flurry of animated talk. Who would go where to get what ingredients? How could we make organic juice ice-lollies? How could we do this? Where could you buy an ice-lolly maker? I was the master of ceremonies, delegating responsibilities, telling people who should go up to the bedroom and spend some special last time with her.

For the next day or so, she was in heaven. Her family gathered round. She smiled, she laughed. She reminisced, she reflected. She sighed, she dozed. It was a weird choreography. She played the part so well, calming and reassuring those who could not hold back the tears, sharing childhood experiences with her sisters. She looked beautiful. Her face showed no signs of the disease. The diet had made her skin silky, almost translucent. She looked more ready to be married than to die.

And yet, although this was an overwhelming experience, and these were the most memorable days of my life, I grew weary of death. On the Saturday afternoon, I took time out to watch the English FA football final. It was time for life, time for some excitement, time to take a break from the tedium of death. Now, looking back, it feels strange, as if I had committed an act of betrayal. How could I? While the love of my life lay dying upstairs, I was downstairs caught up watching men kick a ball around a field.

Life is beautiful and cruel, and death can be banal. I remember seeing a photo once of a group of Nazi soldiers sitting up on a bank, eating, talking and reading as below them prisoners were being lined up to be shot and fall into the pit that had been dug. Another one bites the dust.

And so it came to Sunday, her last day. She was bright and cheerful, sitting up in bed talking as if we were all going to go for a picnic. There were things to be done, people to see. The day began with an art project. The week before, our new neighbours, Ivan and Joanelle, had called in with a bunch of red tulips and yellow lilies for her. I had put them in a vase across from the end of the bed. Each day she remarked on their fading beauty. She loved how, at the beginning of the week, they had been young, pert and tight, how they opened up slowly each day revealing their inner colour and how, now, no matter how much fresh water they were given, they were beginning to wilt and droop.

When Arron arrived in after breakfast, she insisted that he get her camera and take a photo of the fading flowers. She checked the image on the camera. She was not satisfied. It had to be from where she was. Because she could not move easily, Arron had to take off his shoes, come into my side of the bed, and lie down beside her. She made him take numerous shots before she was happy. It was important to get the image right.

I laughed and did what I could to help, but inside I was crying. It was more madness. What was the point in all this? For whom was this being done? Was it for her? Was it for me? Did she really believe that it would have significance for someone beyond her death? Was it because she was an artist? They are not like ordinary people; they continue being artists right up to the moment they die.

Waiting for death is like waiting for birth. There is the same feeling of wondering when will it come: tonight, today, tomorrow? In the kitchen, there was the attempt to carry on as normal; everyone moving quietly, dancing apologetically round each other, afraid to laugh and be happy, making light superficial talk for fear that a wrong word would cause the emotional dam to burst.

Upstairs, Aileen was having none of it. Her parents, Paddy and Anne, came in during the afternoon. Paddy was, as always, pragmatic.

'How are you doing, Aileen?'

'Not too good Dad.'

'Are you doing the breathing exercises I told you about?'

'I'm trying Dad, but it's not so easy.'

Paddy was always full of advice as to how to live a good life.

'You've got to get rid of the stress. You've got to breathe in from the stomach.'

Paddy was a Dale Carnegie man. He believed passionately in positive thinking, to the extent that he believed that cancer was all in the mind. We become beset with worries, fears and anxieties. The mind turns in on itself and creates enormous stress on the body. The only way to get rid of the stress was through deep breathing. He was furious when the doctors told Aileen she had cancer. He was convinced that the worry and stress accelerated the spread of the disease. He believed that if she had never been told that she had cancer, that if she had done her stomach breathing as he had told her, she would not be dying. Indeed he was adamant that even though she had only hours to live, there was still a chance of turning things round.

The extended family began to drift away as the evening came to an end. As they left, there was a feeling of sadness as they wondered if they would ever see Aileen again. The night nurse arrived, the angel of death. She was very skilled at what she did. She slipped in and out of the bedroom now and again, checking, testing, taking pulses and temperatures, looking for signs of deterioration. She presided gently. She spent most of the night sitting out on the stairs reading *The Grapes of Wrath*.

And so it came down to Arron, Olwen, and me.

She was coming in and out of consciousness. I kept talking and talking to her, holding her hand, reassuring her. But what could I say? Don't worry, everything is going to be just fine? I used to say that when we were flying and the plane shuddered from hitting an air pocket. Aileen hated flying. Now she was crashing down to death. I had no lines prepared. I reached out for hackneyed old metaphors. I tried a variation on an old story. She was a passionate gardener. I described the patio downstairs, the shower of colour from the potted plants, the begonias that Carol had put in, the roses, the path down past the pond, the lilac, and then turning right through the arch of honeysuckle, out into the far end of the garden, along the path by the lawn with the fuchsia, alliums and peonies to the left and on down to her studio. I told her that this time she would have to go into her studio on her own. I could not go with her, but she would be happy there, back where she always longed to be. I continued with the make believe. I told her that our Luke, our young son who had died seventeen years previously, was waiting for her. He was with God, as she would soon be, and I would be there with them both in the blink of an eye. I talked and talked.

Eventually I stopped talking and began singing 'Some Enchanted Evening' from *South Pacific*. It had become our song. When I finished, she held my hand a little tighter. She gave me a scornful look.

'It's not fair,' she said, 'I can't dance.'

She seemed to be slipping even further away. She was sinking into wet sand. About one o'clock, she raised herself from the pillow, shc rcachcd out for my hand and she looked me in the eye and spoke quietly and assuredly with a short pause between each phrase.

'I love you, I love you, I love you.'

It was as if, before sinking, she summoned up all her strength to haul herself back to the surface. There was only one thing she wanted to say before she died.

She went into an even deeper space, but she was still fighting. I was moistening her lips with a swab. At one stage she grabbed the swab between her teeth. She would not let go. She held on for minutes. The night nurse said I was lucky it was not my finger. For the next three hours I lay beside her, again listening for every breath, again not knowing which would be her last.

Around half past six, the nurse began to get ready to leave. She gave Aileen a final injection. She said she did not think it would be long. I asked if I would have time to make some coffee. She said yes, but not to delay. Arron and Olwen had gone to bed. I went in and wakened them, told them to keep watch, and went down to the kitchen. I was only downstairs for a couple of minutes when they called for me to come back up. Her breathing had changed. She was gasping. Suddenly the breathing stopped. I cried out in pain. I looked to Arron and Olwen. There was nothing to be said. She was staring deep into space but there was nothing more to see. I closed her eyes. She was gone.

2

The madness is over. I lie awake, where she used to lie, wondering what has happened. I am numb, somewhere between life and death. How can I survive? Do I want to? I go back, over and over those last days, trying to remember the details. What did I feel? What did I say? What did I do? What exactly happened, when, and where? Who was present? Who was missing?

It is a false sense of control. It is as if I believe that if I get all the details right, all the events in chronological order, everything and everyone in their proper time and place, that somehow I will have understood it all. I could bring neatness to the chaos. The reality is that I am at the edge of the abyss into which Aileen fell. No mastery of the details, of what was done when and where, will make it meaningful. But there is pleasure and satisfaction in raking through the ashes, remembering how it was.

It was relentlessly beautiful that last week. I was still quite innocent. I really had no idea of what was happening. I was losing her. I knew she was dying, but

I could not grasp the enormity of it all, so I turned my back to the dreadful vista. Ever since I was a child, like many others, I had this fear of being left behind. It was a fear of losing my mother. Even when she went into town shopping, I could not stop thinking that she would never return. I wanted everything to stay the same. I hated it when family, friends and neighbours went on holiday. I hated being on my own.

I never got over this fear of loss. Every time Aileen went away on business, I longed for the day and then the hour that she would return. In between time, I lived in hope that she would surprise me by coming home early. The sound of her car in the driveway, the turning of the key in the door, the clanking of heels on the tiles, the entrance into the study, the smile, the elation. But this time, there would be no surprise. Death is the end of hope.

I really did not know she was going to go so soon. It was the previous weekend, the Saturday. I was sitting out on the patio, in the late afternoon sunshine. I heard her coming in. She had been out to lunch with her parents. She was not able to drive any more, so I had left her out, and they left her home. She was as radiant as ever, smiling, talking excitedly about her day out. She was full of hope, asking what I had been up to, who had brought the tulips and lilies, what was happening the next day. Were Charles and Vivienne still on to come over for a game of cards the next day? Were they still going on holiday to Spain? Will we get them to stay to supper? Would there be time to cut back the ivy on the wall? It really has become overgrown.

Life seemed to be as it always had been. Aileen forever busy, coming and going, getting and spending, making plans, talking animatedly about her day. Did I not see the bent, hobbled figure struggling with her stick? Did I not see how frail and weak she was? Did I not see that she would be dead in just a week? Did she?

Should I get up? What is the point? I feel as if I have been caught in a cage of time and space. I am here now, it is so real, and yet it all seems so meaningless and arbitrary, the chances of life. How did it come to this? I came out of nowhere, met Aileen, created meaning, made love, and now it is gone. In the blink of an eye, it was all over. And so as she used to stare out the window facing into death, I now stare facing into meaninglessness.

Ever since the day death came out of the blue and staked a claim on Aileen, we lived somewhere between fear and hope, always making believe in the future. In those last few days, as in the last few years, we were like two eager children who, defying logic, keep building their sandcastle even as the incoming tide is washing it away. I feel completely broke. All the love and meaning that I had invested in Aileen was gone. I had lost all my love savings. Maybe if I had been more cautious, maybe if I had not put all my love into the one basket, I would not feel so lost and broke now?

Am I angry? Do I blame her for all this? Was it all her fault for going off and dying? I cannot get over the wonderful paradox of being. The more love and meaning we create, the greater the sense of loss. My mother told me often enough that if you play with fire, you will die by fire. Dave, an American friend, told me that if you let the fire of love grow too strong, you will get emotionally burnt. Maybe I should have listened to them.

I can see her the following day, making it down to the garden, out onto the patio, for the last time. She wore her long, flowing, cream summer dress. She was determined to look beautiful, to take pleasure in every last minute of life that she had. We had been reading the papers after breakfast. She became quiet, deep in thought. She turned to me and said she wanted to paint. She wanted me to set up her easel on the patio. She wanted to work with water-colours, to paint the pond, and the flowers, shrubs and pots that surrounded it. It was as if she wanted to take this image with her into eternity. She told me where to find the paints and paper in her studio. I would have to bring down her chair from the bedroom. She had to be upright and comfortable. I would have to put out the umbrella: the sun would be too much in the early afternoon.

And so I did. She sat and stared intently at the scene before her. It was as if she wanted to sense it, to feel it emotionally, to immerse herself in it, before she attempted to capture it. And then slowly, weighed down by the amount of morphine, she lifted the brush, dipped it in the water-colour, and brought it to the paper. It was a struggle. Many times, she became frozen in time. The brush might remain in the paint. It might stop half way to the paper and, having arrived, it might rest for ages on the paper before being lifted back to the paint. There was nothing I could do to help. And, slowly, the image took shape. It was another still life. In the last months, when the cancer had spread to her spine, she had started painting still lifes. This was her last. But she only got half way. She became too tired. She dozed.

Charles and Vivienne arrived. They were going on holiday the next week, but they were apprehensive. Nothing was said, but there was a fear that they would never see her again. Over the last number of years we had developed the practice of playing bridge, drinking wine and eating supper together on a Friday night. It had become a way of being, a simple pleasure. There were many times I proclaimed at the end of one of those evenings that a good game of cards with good friends was as good as it gets.

I took away the easel and paints, and replaced them with the card table. Charles and Vivienne arrived, and soon we were playing our game of bridge, chatting away, making our bids, as if nothing had changed: one heart, pass, two spades, pass, four hearts. As in most card games, one of the moments of excitement in bridge is picking up the thirteen cards to see what you have been dealt. There is a tingling sensation when you see lots of colour or length in one suit. Sometimes, if you are really lucky, you get good cards all night. Other times you are out of luck. Aileen did not get a decent hand all evening. Nothing was said. Nobody could say the obvious.

As always, she played with Charles. He got some good cards. This meant that even when they, as a team, made a successful bid, she was always the dummy. She sat silently and smiled, and we all said nothing.

And as it had been with the painting, so it was with her card playing. She would reach out and select a card but, dazed by the morphine, she would freeze in mid moment, as if someone had pressed her pause button. She became like a mime artist, moving graciously but irregularly, holding the cards in front of her. And so we sat in silence, watching her, willing her on, waiting, wondering, and then the relief as she carefully put the card on the table.

I could go on and on, looking back into the past, remembering all that was so beautiful and sure, all that I have lost. I know there is so much to be done, so much life to live. But I seem to have lost faith in life, again. The moment I relax my guard, the moment I begin to trust life, it turns round and bites me. I go over and over that last week. I go over and over my life. Back into the past, gathering the pieces of my life, trying to fit them together, hoping that some clear image will emerge. But I need a hand. How can I do this on my own? I have returned to being the frightened child I always was, afraid of being alone.

3

Can I see how it all came to be? Can I hold what was intensely private and personal, that element of pure being immersed in experience, beyond language and yet, at the same time, understand how everything I did and said was part of a web of meaning and culture that had been spun over centuries and would continue on without me, catching babies as they came from the womb and making them into individuals who think they are unique and yet are nothing more than insignificant, arbitrary products of time.

Can I see the arbitrariness of my existence? I grew up in a space and time, in a culture and social class not of my own choosing. I see myself back in Ardtona, the big house in south Dublin in which I grew up. It was one of those estate houses dotted across the Irish landscape. It had been built by the Wallers, members of the Anglo-Irish landed gentry, a huge grey-stone building, with wings and annexes. It had three floors with a large, walled garden at the back. We rented the middle floor in the main house.

I was born into a professional middle-class family. I grew up with my sister Judy, who was fifteen when I was born, and my brother, Maurice, who is five years older than me. It was a cold house but I felt warm, comfortable and happy. The middle floor had grand rooms with high ceilings, big marble fireplaces and enormous sash windows: most of these were jammed shut and had never been opened. In summer we lorded over the house and garden. In winter we huddled around the fireplace in the living room, and used a mixture of paraffin oil fire heaters and hot-water bottles to keep warm in the bedrooms.

Dad was the keeper of the oil heaters. He kept turning them up or down, checking the tank level, trimming the wicks. He was also the bread man. At night, when we had gone to bed, he would bake a loaf of brown soda bread. He was a big man with soft hands. I craved for his touch, but he shied away from intimacy and physical affection. He was difficult to get close to, but he was kind and gentle. He never raised his voice to me or hit me, but on the other hand he rarely touched or hugged me. I knew that he cared for me, but I wanted him to hold me, to wrap me up in his arms and tell me how much he loved me.

As a young boy, when I woke up from a nightmare and was too scared to stay in my bedroom, I would immediately think of going to him: he was my saviour. But I was in the left wing of the house, and to get to Dad I had to journey in the dark through large, silent rooms. It was frightening, reaching out into the black night with my hands, into an abyss full of ghosts, evil and the unknown.

I had to feel my way out of my bed, across the bedroom, to the tall door that led into the study. I had to cross through it, picking my way through the chairs and table. The door opened out into the long hall that ran the length of the house. Slowly but surely I would edge my way past the first chair, the dresser, then the second chair. The greatest danger lurked between the dresser and the second chair. When I was playing hide-and-seek with my brother, Maurice, I used to hide there. This was where the boogie man would be, waiting to pounce. Once I came to the end of the dresser, I knew the pillar in the middle of the hall was not far off. The door to my parents' bedroom was to the left. I would pause for a second, and then make a mad dash for it. Dad's bed was nearest the door. I slid quietly in beside him, not saying a word. He always slept on his right side. And, as always, as soon as he felt me behind him, his right hand came up over his shoulder to reach out and hold on to mine. I would hold on tightly until I fell back asleep.

I spent most of my life trying to be different from my father, only to realise more and more how similar I am. It is not just in having the same genetic make-up, the same eyes, nose, face, hands and feet. It is in little things like my mannerisms, smile, laughter, frown. It is the same way of talking, the same way of holding and presenting myself, the same disposition, the detached, sceptical, quizzical expression. Most of all I wonder if I am really just my father dressed in different cultural clothes. And if the difference is that small, how different am I from his father, and his father before him? It would be great to gather all my forefathers together and spend some time sitting, talking, walking, examining each other, our bodies and minds, seeing what was similar and different. Each of us convinced of their difference, and yet all of us so similar.

I would especially like to meet my grandfather. I have no image of him. There was no photo of him in Ardtona. Dad never talked about him. It was Uncle Anthony, Dad's brother, who told me his story. My grandfather was an engineer and architect. His success came when he designed a number of the large, plush houses in Foxrock, the new, leafy, bourgeois suburb of Dublin in the early years of the twentieth century. He was in business with a Polish man. He was married with seven children, and lived in a big Georgian house on Mount Street.

I try to imagine my grandfather, this man of my being. I want to know if he had the same quirky sense of humour, the same mercurial, unpredictable way of behaving. Did he keep his innermost thoughts to himself? Did he show his emotions? But I can only see him as a type, as a man caught in Irish time and space, of a particular class. I see him as a well-dressed, professional man parading through Joycean Dublin, moving in elite circles, being polite, doffing his hat to women, voicing his opinions among his friends, partaking in the pleasures of life.

Uncle Antony was a great man for embellishment. He told me of the day that he and his brother, Maurice, were playing upstairs in the bedroom in Mount Street when, suddenly, there was a huge commotion down below. They ran downstairs to find out what was happening. As they descended, they met soldiers running up the stairs. The house had been commandeered by the army. There were soldiers everywhere; sergeants barking out orders. The family was corralled into the kitchen and living room. It was Easter Monday, 1916.

A year after this intrusion, everything seems to have been going very well: his marriage was sound, and the last of his seven children had been born. Business was good but, out of the blue, his Polish colleague disappeared. Granddad discovered he had been embezzling the company's funds. It went bust and, having lost all his money and reputation, he had little choice but to join the army. He was posted to Egypt.

The camp to which he was sent was being devastated by malaria. He came up with the idea of building a false swamp to which the mosquitoes would be attracted and then exterminated. It seems a simple idea, but it got him promotion and an OBE. He should have come home from the war with his reputation regained, if not enhanced. Unfortunately, when in Egypt, he became infected with syphilis. Uncle Anthony worked in films and liked to create a bit of drama, so, when he told me this story, he hesitated at the end, looked over, and said that he had heard it was from the young men he frequented.

He seems to have been a bit of lad my granddad, and a bit of a gambler. The first night of his honeymoon on board a cruise liner, he stayed on in the bar after his wife had gone down to bed. He got into a card game. Having lost all his money, he went down below and persuaded his wife to take off her engagement ring so that he could show it to this jeweller to whom he had been describing it. He lost that as well.

At least he was brave enough to tell my grandmother that he had syphilis. She seems to have been forgiving, but her mother was not. She insisted that if her daughter let him inside the front door, she would be cut off from the family and any inheritance. And so, the day came when granddad arrived home in a horse and cab. He knocked on the door. His wife went out to talk to him. Uncle Anthony and the other children looked on from the sitting-room window. There was a heated scene on the doorstep. He pleaded to be let in to see the children. His wife pleaded with him not to. Eventually he did the gentlemanly thing and left. He went back to Blackpool, where he had been stationed on his return from Egypt.

There was an attempted reconciliation and his wife and kids went to Blackpool for a while, but it did not work out. She came home and, while her mother did welcome her back, there were strict conditions. She was given a measly weekly allowance which was paid out through her brother, a priest. But her mother seems to have been a Victorian dragon, intent on teaching her daughter a lesson. My grandmother could not make ends meet. Eventually she was forced to put two of her sons into an orphanage for a year. It was only when the year's sentence had been served that her mother relented and increased her allowance.

I try to imagine my granddad, gradually losing his health and perhaps his mind. I want to go back in time, to talk to him, to reassure him, to forgive and hug him. Things seem to have gone from bad to worse. Every week his batman went down to the local bank to collect the money for the soldiers' wages. One week he did not come back. Granddad was court-martialled. He was transferred to London where he died a couple of years later. Dad was the only member of the family who attended his funeral.

In the early days, when I was young and things were normal, Dad seemed to have an idyllic life. In the 1950s, Ireland was a European backwater, wracked by poverty, over-breeding and emigration. But it was a good place to be for a Catholic professional man. He had met Mum in the early 1930s, and they had married and moved into Ardtona. Mum was almost forty-five years old when she gave birth to me. I was referred to as an afterthought. Following the tradition, my brother, Maurice, being the first born son, should have been given Dad's name, 'Thomas'. But his brother, uncle Maurice, was on a trip home from Canada during the July when Maurice was born. And so, in recognition of his visit home, Mum and Dad christened their first born son 'Maurice'. When I was born, it was time to make amends, and not only to call me 'Thomas', but 'Francis'. Growing up with the exact same Christian names as my father had its costs. Given that he was six feet three inches, and I was so small, it was probably inevitable that he would be called 'Big Tom' and I would be dubbed 'Little Tom'.

Being a good Catholic meant that professional men like Dad could not be overly ambitious. People got to the top of their profession in the same way that a priest became a bishop or a bishop the Pope. Everyone played the game of humility. It was a Catholic world of parsimony and piety; of making do and not wanting. Self-indulgence, desire and naked ambition were mortal sins. Class distinction revolved more around honour and lifestyle than material success. Families like ours may have lived in grand houses, but they were cold spaces in which curtains and carpets were threadbare, and chairs and couches were worn back to the springs. We may have been wealthy but, for Catholic appearances, we were forced to live a life of genteel poverty.

Dad must have been good at playing the game, as he managed to become President of the Royal Institute of Architects of Ireland. He was the senior architect in Vincent Kelly, one of the big architectural firms. There may have been stresses at work, but I was never aware of them. He had leisurely, regular practices.

After breakfast in bed, he would rise at 8.30 and drive into the office on Merrion Square. At 1.00, he would drive back home for lunch. After lunch he would read the paper, doze, and drive back into work. He would leave work around 6.00 and go to drink whiskey with his professional friends in O'Briens in Leeson Street. He worked on Saturdays until lunchtime, when he went to drink whiskey in Elm Park golf club. He never took work home with him. He devoted most of the weekend to his passion, working in the garden.

I never thought of him as a holy man. And yet, he seems to have designed a lot of churches, which in those days in Catholic Ireland were big commissions. He went to Mass on Sunday, read the Bible in bed at night, and said the family rosary, but he did not have the same religious devotion as my mother. He was not the one who dragged us up and down to the church for Mass, benediction, devotions, novenas, missions and whatever else was going on. He was not the one who brought us to our knees to say the rosary every Sunday night and every night in Lent.

However, what he did every Lent was organise the Institute of Architects' annual retreat to the Jesuits in Milltown Park. It was a typical Irish affair. It lasted two days, and the evening they went in they all met up in O'Briens and retired back there when it was all over.

Dad made one big mistake in his life. He left Vincent Kelly, one of the big architectural firms in Dublin, and went out on his own. He felt he was doing most of the work, but that Vincent Kelly was getting most of the credit and more of the income. But while Dad may have had a good eye for design, he had no idea how to run a business. He did all right in the first year, but as a single architect he was not able to get big commissions. He survived on small local government contracts and the ESB.

His big mistake was compounded by opening his office across the road from O'Briens. Being independent, friends began to ask him to do designs for houses and extensions. He obliged, but never asked to be paid. It was as if asking them for money was dishonourable. There were nights when I would pass by their bedroom and I could hear Mum pleading with him to send out fees. And so it got worse. Perhaps feeling ashamed for not having paid him, his friends plied him with drink. Every Christmas, dozens of bottles of whiskey and hundreds of cartons of cigarettes would be delivered out to Ardtona. Slowly but surely he sank into whiskey. Within a couple of years, his business folded. Soon he was broke. Without his sister, Joan, and then, later, the love and support of Judy and Maurice, we would have gone under.

It all happened rather quickly. One year there was talk of us flying out to Spain for a summer holiday. A couple of years later, I had to get a summer job as a butcher's messenger boy in Meehan's in Rathmines. I lied to get the job. I was supposed to be fourteen years old. I was only thirteen. I pretended that I wanted to leave school and become an apprentice butcher. My main task was to cycle a big black bike with a big wicker basket at the front. I had to deliver packages of meat to the middle-class homes of the area. On Saturday mornings, the basket was full to the brim, and mounting and dismounting was scary. Living the lie of being a butcher boy meant having to put on a Dublin accent and meet up with the other delivery boys to swap gossip, tell jokes, and smoke fags. Although I had been smoking for a year or so, I was not used to the unfiltered Players and Aftons that were the favoured cigarettes of hardened delivery boys. The style of smoking involved taking deep drags down into the bottom of the lungs and stomach. The first few Saturday mornings I was dizzy with the smoke. I could not be seen to wobble, so I had to wait behind and watch as the lads demonstrated their skill at running and jumping onto the bikes.

I detested the abattoir at the back of the shop. I was sent down in the first couple of weeks to be blooded, to arrive as the slaughtering was under way. It was a world of burly men draped in special aprons, walking between bright red guts and carcasses, bringing in the next victim, holding them down and putting the stun gun to their head. My last job every Saturday evening was to go to the vegetable shop and get a bag of the left over leaves from cauliflowers and cabbages, then take them down to the shed behind the abattoir and feed the cattle waiting to be slaughtered early Monday morning. I would cry as I fed them, their big tongues reaching out to take the leaves from my hand.

I went quite quickly from being proud of Dad to feeling ashamed. The garden, the paradise in which I used to lose myself, gradually became a wilderness. In the summer of '67, I tried, in vain, to retrieve it. I wanted to walk along the paths through the ordered magic of fir trees, fruit trees, bushes, flowers, and lawns. I hacked away at the overgrowth, dug out the weeds from the flower beds, and had huge bonfires. It was a waste of time.

Dad had a peculiar Victorian attitude, not just to sex, but to his body. While it was part of Catholic prudery, it may also be related to the sexual stigma of his father dying of syphilis. In some respects, he was a very clean man. He washed himself at the sink every morning, splashing water around his upper body after shaving. But he rarely had a bath. Every two to three months, Mum would go on a campaign on a Sunday morning to get him out of bed into a bath. It would have been easier trying to bathe a cat. But it was also an opportunity for her to get his vest and long johns off him. He wore these all day and, when going to bed, put his pyjamas on over them.

I never saw him naked. One morning, as I came charging down the hall and he was coming back from a bath, his pyjama bottoms dropped to the floor. I was startled by the large snake that emerged from the bush of hair and the huge red-veined balls that dangled from below. He was mortified.

Like many other Catholic Irish men of his time, he was sexually and emotionally deeply repressed. When we got a television in the early sixties, he took delight in watching Eva Gabor in the American sitcom *Green Acres*. She was a beautiful doll: he could play with her, she was unreal.

However, when the BBC began to put on television plays reflecting real life, and when there was any scene in which a couple kissed deeply as a build-up to real sex, Dad would become enormously agitated. He would go puce red with embarrassment and, when he could no longer contain himself, he would rise quickly from his armchair, cross over to the television and turn it off, saying 'I am not watching this rubbish,' leaving the rest of the family sitting in silence, cut off from the world.

In those troubled times, Ferdie became Dad's source of comfort and consolation. He used to say that he was the most civilised person in the house: he never gave out or complained and he was always welcoming. He was a big black and white dog, a mix between an English setter and a boxer. We all had a fondness for Ferdie. He was his own dog, a dog's dog. He was a source of consolation, amusement and happiness. There were many shameful and funny incidents. He wandered far from Ardtona, into neighbours' back gardens and into their bins. His favourite occupation in the afternoon was to go up to the main Dundrum road and lie in wait for some old dear driving slowly and nervously down the road, keeping well into the kerb. Ferdie would tear off after the car, barking furiously at the front wheel. After a hundred yards, he would give up, find a lamppost and nonchalantly piss against it before idling back to take up his position at the top of the road, waiting for his next victim.

It was, of course, dangerous. He got knocked down numerous times. When he was 18, blind and almost deaf, but his nose still functioning, he went up to the Dundrum road, walked out in front of a milk lorry and got squashed to death. Mum phoned to say that Mrs Nunan had seen it happen. She had dragged his body to the side of the road. Mum wanted me to come over from Terenure and bring him home. I did not have a car and so I went over on my bike. I had to stretch him across the back carrier and walk him home, past the spot where he waited for his cars. I went round the back of the house and dug a plot in the garden, under the fir trees, in among the lupins and asters. There were no prayers, just memories and tears.

I have wondered about this fondness I have for dogs. I become attached to them. I loved when Dad talked about the dogs of his childhood. It was as if they were members of his family. Ferdie became the mediator between Dad and I; we talked about each other through him. It was as if he was a child for whom we had to care. He would tell me tales of Ferdie's encounters with other dogs, cats, birds and humans. He would defend him against complaints from Mum. He would feed him secret treats, and towards the end of the day Ferdie would nuzzle in between Dad's legs to have his head rubbed.

I had to invent ways of getting close to Dad, getting him to touch me and show his love. In the evenings, as he sat watching television, I would plead that I needed a back scratch. I would sit down on the arm of his chair. I would lift up my vest, shirt and jumper and his hand would slide up my back. We would both continue to watch the television. I deliberately sought a scratch in the middle of programmes like *Green Acres*, *Mister Ed*, *The Beverly Hillbillies* or *The Jack Benny Show* so that we could both have a laugh together as he scratched away. He seemed to cultivate his fingernails so that they would be ideal for the back scratching, just over the edge of the skin of the finger. His technique was simple. It involved a minimal but continuous motion with the four fingers on his right hand. He would start up on the upper right hand side and move slowly across. When he reached my left hand shoulder, he dropped down to the next level and inched his way across. My task was to move and arch my back in rhythm to his fingers. It was a tango. At certain times, and with an appropriate 'ah yes there,' I would call on him to work on one spot in particular. When it was all over, without any formal recognition that anything had happened, I would get up, pull my clothes down, and say 'Thanks, Dad.' Sometimes I scratched his back, but it was quick, short and rather perfunctory, and it only happened when he genuinely felt itchy.

One summer evening I walked over to the local pub with him. We sat upstairs at the bar. It was 1979, and Aileen and I were leaving soon to go to the States to do graduate studies. Arron was only six months old. I had no idea when we would be back. I was fearful that I might not see him again. I decided to take the bull by the horns, and so, as we finished our first drink, I looked at him long and softly and smiled. I told him about how some years previously when following a competition in the local golf club, I had, out of the corner of my eye, seen his face in the crowd at the far side of the green, and how I had realised that although I recognised him, I did not know him, that he was as much a stranger as a father.

'You know, you are going to die and I will have never really known you.'

He looked away. He took his time. Slowly, he looked me in the eye, over his half-rimmed glasses that perched at the end of his nose.

'Are you going to have another drink or not?'

A few weeks later, I was in the the Bottle Tower, our local pub in Churchtown, with our friends Nigel and Angela. I got a phone call from Mum saying that Dad had been found on the 14 bus and that they could not revive him. I ran out of the pub, and the bus was stopped across the road. When I got to him he was mumbling incoherently. He had got on the bus a couple of hours earlier and, as we found out, had a massive stroke. The bus conductor tried to revive him and, although Dad was seventy-five years old and it was only midday, assumed that he was drunk. The bus had gone in and out of town three times before the conductor decided to do something. He searched his pocket and found some identification and had phoned home. Dad died six days later.

I have often wondered what went through his mind that day as he was slumped in the bus, looking out the window, going back in and out of town, with the world passing by down below and people gazing at him as they came up and down the stairs. What was it like to be caught in his body without his mind, unable to speak, a frightened human capsule hurtling through time and space?

I can see now, when I stop deluding myself, that I am not that much different from Dad. I may live a different life, know different people, do different things, but I see more and more that I have the same character, the same quirks and foibles, the same sense of humour. I may have a different body, but I have the same emotional interior. All of this writing and talking, trying to say what cannot be said, is an attempt to break the silence in which he was trapped.

4

Aileen's and my bed was never really just our bed. The children always seemed to have equal rights of access. They climbed in and out whenever they wanted. There was no sense of shame, awkwardness or embarrassment. It was a regular event for them to come in and crawl around, up and down the bed in between us.

My mother never let me into her bed while she was in it. But in the morning, if I was in Dad's bed, as soon as she got up I would leave Dad and climb in under her blankets. She did not use sheets. Maybe it was a penitential practice, maybe it was to save on the laundry bill. The blankets were old and worn. It was a harsh environment, but the smells were divine. Lying in her bed was as close as I ever came to physically possessing her. I could drink her in through my nose. It was a heady mixture of stale body odours, perfume and tobacco.

I never met my mother's parents. Like Dad, she did not talk about them much. I have no idea how much of them I have inherited. However, it was said often enough – and I have come to recognise it myself – that there is more of a Muldoon than an Inglis in me, especially in my physical features. So despite my fascination with granddad Inglis, it may be that more of how I have come to be the way I am was derived from grandmother Muldoon. She seems to have been a nice woman; Mum never implied anything otherwise. Like grandmother Inglis, she too had seven children. Unlike many other women in Ireland at the time, she could afford them.

The Muldoons, like the Inglises, were urban bourgeois, but unlike them they left a visual testimony. There is a photo of the entire family. It is one of those posed photos taken by a professional photographer. Everyone is, as Uncle Oliver, one of the sons, would say, 'in their best bib and tucker'. They are gathered around a bench in the bottom of the garden in Clonskeagh. Four of the boys are in suits, the oldest boy, Sean, in his school uniform, the two girls, Mum and her sister, Maureen, are in plain summer frocks. Nobody is smiling. This is serious business. This is a formal photo of a successful Dublin bourgeois man and his family: it is right and fitting that they be immortalised in history. Granddad Muldoon stands at the back, tall, stern and erect, looking out into the world with his wife and children gathered round him.

He was undoubtedly a success. He wrote numerous books and pamphlets, most of them about the work of government and public policy. He also published a novel, a story about a rigged convention in Dublin. He grew up in Dromore, County Tyrone, became a barrister, and then became involved in Irish nationalist politics. He was a Redmondite, and was elected as an MP for the Irish Parliamentary Party for thirteen years from 1905. He would have been an MP while my mother was growing up. He went back to the law and, in later life, became Registrar of Lunacy in Ireland.

He was wealthy enough to send all his children to the top schools in Dublin. He also made the strategic decision to invest in his daughters' education by sending them to 'finishing' school in Belgium. Mum did not talk much about her experience with the nuns. But she did tell me, more than once, that when the girls were having a bath they had to wear a cotton chemise to protect themselves from seeing themselves.

Shortly after leaving school, Mum went off to Czechoslovakia to work as a governess for a local count. She learned to smoke there. She said it was to fend off the mosquitoes. She also fell in love. During her time off, she took to walking down to the local small town. She was a beautiful young woman. She began to pay visits to the local chemist. They began to walk out together. I have no idea how old he was, of what was said and done. However, it appears that the excitement of being away from home and, at the same time, of being alone and rather homesick in the count's castle, led her to fall in love. They made plans. She came home, told her parents about him, and sought their permission to marry. I can imagine her leaving him, travelling across Europe by train and boat full of hope and trepidation.

Granddad immediately put his foot down. There was no way his daughter was going to go and marry some chemist in Czechoslovakia. Maybe he thought it was for her own good, maybe it was because he had invested so much in her education, maybe it was because she had fallen in love with a Jew. Mum was forbidden to return. She wrote to her lover. He wrote back. They continued writing long letters, three or four times a year. He married. I don't know how many children he had, but his daughter wrote to Mum during the years he spent in a Nazi concentration camp. After the war he returned to writing, and the correspondence kept up until he died.

I was usually at school when the postman came. Every so often a letter would arrive when she was not there, always the same neat handwriting, the foreign stamps and postmarks. It would wait for her on the hall dressser, to be whisked away when she came home. She must have hidden them away or destroyed them. She rarely talked about him or the letters. It was if they were such an intense wound of love that she was afraid to open it up. Once I found one that had been opened, but being in German, it was incomprehensible. But there were many times I would come into her bedroom unexpectedly and she would be sitting on her bed, with a letter open beside her, and she would be crying.

Mum, like Dad, found it difficult to be physically intimate. I have no recollection of sitting on Mum's lap, being cuddled or fondled. And yet she was devoted to me, and I to her. It was a very Catholic form of love, quite platonic and formal, built on a devotion to God and an absolute surrender of the self to family and community. They said of her that she was a saint, and she was. She had a deep sense of love and care. But it was more the love of a nun than a mother. I did not know it then but what I wanted was an earth goddess who would envelop me in her arms. She sacrificed herself, not just for me, but for the family. During the 1960s, when Dad was at the height of his drinking, when there was no money left, she would serve us wonderful meals, cobbled together from the small weekly allowance that dad's sister gave her. While we ate our meat, potatoes and vegetable, she would sit at the end of the kitchen, beside the sink, having her daily ration of packet soup and bread.

Although she did not hug me, she did not castrate me. She let me be. She never used any of those emotional strategies that mothers can employ on their children. She insisted from a young age that I be emotionally independent of her. She never played the role of the sulking, pouting mother, demanding attention and feigning hurt when enough was not given. She took delight in my presence, and she never smothered me.

Mum presented herself as some late Victorian dame. She had been moulded by the nuns. She moved gracefully. She took pride in her beauty. Each morning, in preparation for her pilgrimage to ten o'clock Mass, she spent half an hour sitting in front of the mirror on her dressing table, powdering her face, putting on her lipstick, stopping every now and then to take a puff from the cigarette that waited on the ashtray. Like the Mass, it had its own time and ritual movements.

There was little or no sex in our house, before or after television. I had no conception of how I was conceived. I never saw Mum and Dad in bed together. I never saw them embrace or kiss each other. There were few signs of love and romance. If Mum did get a card for her birthday from Dad, it would often have been bought by my sister, Judy, and Dad would have simply signed 'Dad' under the greeting. It was as if they were living under strict orders to never show any sign of affection. I try to imagine Dad coming in from work, walking up to Mum, holding her eyes with his and, as she fell into his arms, reaching down to kiss her. It is impossible.

Mum was able to make fun of it. Every Friday, Dad used to leave her a cheque for the housekeeping in front of the clock in the living room. She used to tease him and say that as she was a kept woman he might have the decency to leave the cheque under her pillow.

But she too liked a bit of titillation. She felt no shame, and indeed took pleasure, in buying *The Sunday World*. When it came out in the 1970s, it was the first colour Irish tabloid to have busty, scantily clad girls on the front cover with the regular banner headline, 'Are you getting it every Sunday?' When I chided Mum about buying this – she being a good Catholic – she chastised me by telling me that she enjoyed a bit of 'girlie' just as much as anyone else.

I do not know when or why Mum became such a devoted Catholic. Obviously it was in the air at the time. She grew up in a society in which people vied to be more Catholic than their neighbours. I often wonder was it the same in the Soviet Union, people trying to be more Communist, more devoted to The Party, invoking Communist language into their talk, dropping names of members like Mum did priests. She lived in religious time and space. Days were known by the name of saints and Catholic events. Morning, noon and night were marked by different prayers. There were religious seasons, Lent, Easter, May and October devotions, Advent. There were benedictions, missions, novenas to be attended and rosaries to be said. Then there was her voluntary work. Every Thursday afternoon she would walk down to Dundrum and up the hill to Todd Andrews' house where she, and Mary and a host of other good Catholic women, would sew vestments for the missions.

The lasting image I have of Mum is walking up and down to the local Good Shepherd Church. She seemed to always kneel in the same pew. The only excitement in the daily ritual of going to Mass was to find out the celebrant. Catholic priests were celebrities. Mum had her favourites. Most women had a soft spot for Fr Hyland but Mum was fond of Fr Hanlon. He was a well-known artist but he had a raging temper. He detested mothers who brought their babies with them to Mass. He detested more the mothers who could not stop their babies crying. He had a way with them. Once, at an early Sunday Mass, a baby was wailing and he turned from the altar and requested that the woman remove herself and the baby from the church. When she did not comply, he turned round and announced, 'okay, have it your way. If you won't go, I will.' And he did.

He was a priest who demanded respect. I was walking down the road from the church, on my way home with another school pal, when he approached us on the pavement. We were supposed to have greeted him with a smile and a nod of our heads. We didn't. We were caught up in our own world. It was a mistake. And so, just after he passed by, he turned quickly and smacked me across the back of my head, telling me that I should always greet a priest properly.

I have spent a good deal of my life wondering, reflecting and analysing the influence that the Church had on me. I was devoted to Mum and, for years, wanted to emulate her devotion to the Church. When I was young, Jim Nunan and I used to play at being priests. We would take turns at being the altar boy. Later, when I had the opportunity to play the game for real, I was turned down by Fr Hyland. Maybe he knew I would be a failure. I tried to follow in my mother's footsteps, up and down to the church at least once a day. I succeeded in many of my goals. I managed to do the May and October devotions, to go to Mass every day during Lent, but for some reason I never managed to complete the First Nine Fridays.

It was probably Mum's devotion to God and selflessness that enabled her to weather the storm of Dad's collapse into alcoholism. In the 1970s, when he had curtailed his drinking because he did not have any money, Dad and Mum developed a warm, caring relationship. The fear and anxiety she used to have about him began to subside. He began to think and be aware of her, to reach out and show affection through acts of kindness. He managed to haul himself out of the deep depression that besotted him. His humour began to grow. It was as if he had been dead to the world, and slowly he began to sprout new leaves. He did not have to pretend any more. He liked his work, but he hated doing business. Now that he had left this alien world, he spent his days pottering around the house and garden. On Fridays, he would come into town where I worked, and we would go for lunch. Before leaving my office, though, he would always phone Mum to tell her he had arrived safe and sound.

As part of their rediscovery of each other, Mum and Dad took to going out to the pub. It was a little trip away from home to meet neighbours and friends who were rarely invited into the house. The pub was also the place to go for small family celebrations or when something difficult needed to discussed.

A couple of summers after Dad had died, I took Mum up to the local pub and fed her some whiskey. When the moment was right, I popped the question.

'What was sex like with Dad?'

There was a short silence. She looked at me, she pondered, she puffed on her cigarette and said:

'It was short, not very sweet, and not very often.'

Sex was everywhere and nowhere in Ireland in those days. It was something that happened in the middle of the night, like a silent invisible hand. It was felt and remembered, but not talked about. It may have been a source of pleasure, but for many women, and men, it was a source of pain, embarrassment and shame. As on my father's side, there was also sexual shame on my mother's side of the family.

My Auntie Maureen was a funny, mischievous, flirtatious woman. She did not have any children, but she behaved like a child. She was a funny sort of embarrassment. She brought Maurice and I to a film and, discovering that the end of the first screening of the film was still showing, took out her umbrella and put it up to prevent us from finding out the ending.

She was a couple of years younger than Mum. She had married well: a doctor, but she did not know that his high spirits were maintained by helping himself to hard drugs. He died of an overdose. A few years later she met and married Uncle Frank. He was an imperious man with a military bearing. He had been a pilot in the First World War. He told me stories of shooting at Gerry with a pistol from his cockpit. When he left the RAF he joined Shell and became one of their men in China during the 1930s. Uncle Frank loved to talk endlessly about his days in China. He talked in a slow, soporific, pedantic voice. It was as if he had tried to imitate the voice of the BBC World Service, but decided that it was too fast. In between tales of servants from Shanghai, he would stop and puff methodologically on his cigar. He could have bored for Ireland.

Uncle Frank made enough money from his Shell days to retire early. Up to the age of ten, my brother Maurice and I used to visit him and Auntie Maureen in their house in Greystones. We were primed by Mum to be on our best behaviour. He was a stickler for protocol and manners. On the rare occasions when I tried to speak, he would stop me almost immediately and tell me to slow down as he had not understood one word I had said. I would begin again, and this time he would point out all my pronunciation and grammatical mistakes. As he read the morning paper, I would mumble something about going out to the garden. Eventually I would get it right: 'I would like to go out to play in the garden and I shall be back in time for lunch.'

He rarely did anything more than appear at lunch and supper. Lunch was an hour of torture. At home, all

I had to do was ask permission to leave the table. With Uncle Frank, nobody could leave the table until everybody, which meant him, had finished eating. He ate as slowly as he spoke. He used his knife and fork with delicate precision, moving bits of meat, potato and vegetable into position and carefully mounting them onto his fork, all the time talking ponderously about how things were done in his day. When the fork was loaded, he would rest it on the side of his plate and wait until he had come to the end of what he was saying. He would insert it into his mouth. There would be silence as he slowly chomped away. When he had swallowed everything, the ritual would begin again.

Uncle Frank was obsessive about everything. Being childless, he was fearful that Maurice and I would destroy the neat order of his home. There was a time and place for everything. In his workshop, there were shelves of little boxes with various types and sizes of screws and nails, all labelled and in order of size. When he was going away, usually to the RAF club in London, he would take out a typed list of all the clothes and items that he would need. As each was put into the suitcase, he would tick the item on the list lightly with a pencil. When all the items were checked, he would carefully erase each tick with a rubber.

But, underneath it all, Uncle Frank was not what he seemed. One day, in the midst of all his order, coming up to lunchtime, he went to his secret hiding place, took out the erotic black and white photos of nude boys that he had accumulated over the years in London and the Far East, got into his car and drove down to the local boys school. There he waited until the young boys came out, and without getting out of the car, wound down the window and tossed the cards out in front of them. He made his getaway, but his car was spotted and recognised. The gardaí came to his house and he was arrested. The case went to court. Dad and Uncle Paul bribed the journalists not to report the case. Uncle Frank was given the option of leaving the country or going to prison. He and Auntie Maureen went to live in Spain. Nothing was ever said to me at the time. Uncle Frank was another sexual skeleton in the family cupboard.

In 1969, I was teaching in a school in the north of France. My official position was *lecteur en anglais*, which really meant teaching the students proper pronunciation. I got a phone call from my sister, Judy. It was the only phone call I received during my time there. It came through the school office. It was at night. The elderly brother came into the library and told me to come with him immediately. I heard Judy's voice. I trembled with anticipation of deadly news. But it was nothing to do with Dad or Mum, it was about Uncle Frank. I had written to say that he had invited me to take the train up to Calais and the ferry over to Folkstone, where I was to meet him for lunch. It was difficult to read in between the vague lines of advice that Judy gave me.

'You are to say no if he asks you back to his hotel, to stay overnight, or to go back up to London with him,' she said.

'Why?'

'He has his problems. Be wary, he should not be trusted.'

The short phone call had me completely befuddled. I guessed it was something sexual and so, when I arrived, I watched his every move. We ate lunch in a hotel. He was not staying there; he had just travelled down from the RAF club for the day. He suggested a walk. It was in the middle of the walk that we came upon a barber shop, and Frank suggested we might both go and get a haircut. I immediately suspected a ruse. He had hardly any hair to cut. I had heard stories about barbers in England where you could buy condoms. Maybe, I thought, there could be sex as well. I did not know whether to refuse politely, run away, or take the plunge. I took the plunge and it was all harmless: Uncle Frank thought I looked much neater when we came out. He did not like long hair on boys.

5

I can see myself more clearly, all my fears and longings, my idiosyncrasies and inadequacies. I was born into a peculiar sexual culture. I grew up with bodies that were frightened by sex and touch. It was as if the sight of bare flesh, the touch of skin, would unleash some alien creature, a viper that would leap out of my body and devour me. Sex was the devil incarnate.

I grew up ignorant and intrigued about sex. When I was in kindergarten I used to play doctors and nurses with my first girlfriend. We examined each other's bodies. One day we got adventurous and played mummies and daddies. We decided to have a baby. We had no idea how to go about this, but it was obvious that it had something to do with my willie and her gee, so I peed over her.

In school, I spent a lot of time taking the mickey with my male friends. We shouted at girls across the street, 'get them off you' – meaning their knickers – and roared with laughter. Girls were exotic creatures, foreign to us boys. In a world of fine distinctions and divisions, they were as far apart as the English were from us Irish, Catholics from Protestants, the professional middle from the working class.

During the 1950s, the tentacles of Dublin began to reach out to Churchtown. There was a rapid expansion of housing estates. Quite soon there were myriads of young married couples producing young children who had to be educated. The De La Salle Brothers moved in to provide their services. They ran a private fee-paying preparatory school for the middle classes, to which I went, and a national school for working-class children, which was free.

And so it was that I had the privilege, in all my years in preparatory school, to be educated by the same brother. At the beginning of each year we hoped that we would get someone new, but we always got Brother Bernard. He seemed ancient to us, but was probably only in his fifties or sixties. He was in best form in the morning when he paraded up and down the rows as we sang out the morning rosary. He loved to hear the classroom resonate with the devotion of young boys in full prayer. He had a simple strategy: if you did not pray loud enough he beat you. Sometimes in the afternoon, tired from his morning exertions, he would doze off. One afternoon in early summer, he nodded off. Someone in the front row noticed that his tunic had got caught up in his chair. As he slept, we took it in turns to crawl up on the floor to have a look up under his desk to see if you could see his willie. But what if he woke up just as you were under his desk? The solution was simple: you crawled up with a pencil in your mouth and if he woke up at the wrong moment, you dropped it and then stood up and said that you had wanted to use the sharpener that was mounted at the end of his desk and that the pencil had dropped out of your hand. And so the young commandos began to take turns to crawl to the target. In the beginning, in the midst of excitement, it was rumoured you could see his balls. It was nerve-racking but, when it came to my turn, I did not flinch. But it was all very disappointing. All there was to see was a skinny white hairy leg and knobbly knee.

The hunger for sex created vivid imaginations. One Hallowe'en I was sitting in the front row of the large class. It was time to be brave and naughty, to gain honour and respect among my classmates. I tore off a piece from my copybook and wrote 'Don't kiss your girlfriend tonight there is danger under her lips.' It got back as far as Michael Flaherty, whose roaring laugh brought the attention of Brother Bernard. He grabbed the piece of paper. He wanted to know who had written such filth. I was fingered. He took out his leather and started to wallop my hands. Suddenly, he stopped. He realised that this was beyond the normal offence and decided he would have to call in the Headmaster, Brother Florence.

They both stormed back into the classroom. Flory grabbed me by the ear and pulled me down the stairs into his office. He was ranting. He could not contain his rage. He fumbled for the cane behind the door. He was a small, fat man. He lashed into me. He was sweating heavily. The lashing and running up and down the stairs had taken their toll. After a number of lashes, he stopped for a breather. It was my moment of salvation. He gasped.

'How could you write such a thing?'

'A boy from High School told me,' I said.

I had played the Protestant card. It worked like magic. It was a complete lie, but he believed me. Another innocent Catholic boy had been contaminated by the Protestants. It was the only obvious explanation. He calmed down. He did not apologise or forgive me. Instead, he talked about keeping bad company.

I grew up with lots of Protestants. The Taylors and the Prices lived on Ardtona Avenue. We all played together, but they were different. They went to different churches and schools. They were not educated by the same weird old men in black. But there was something else. They did not seem to be weighed down by their bodies and sex. They were confident and exuberant, exotic and erotic. I often wondered what it was like to be a brother, to have been whisked away from home as a young teenager because someone told you that you had a vocation, and then realise that not only were you unlikely ever to have sex, but you could never mention the subject. What did the brothers fantasise about? Did they fantasise about Protestants like I did?

Mum used to tell me that 'a little bit of knowledge does an awful lot of harm.' I think this is what she had in mind when she decided it was time for me to know the facts of life. I was about twelve. I came home from school one day and found a Catholic leaflet about sex. I was so excited just to see the word sex printed on a page. I had no idea how it got onto my bed. I thought, quite naïvely, that it was meant for Maurice, and that she had left it on my bed by accident. I dashed off to the bathroom, locked the door and began reading.

It was all very unsatisfying. I thought I would get aroused. Instead, I became confused. It was full of vague, opaque language. The climax was a real disappointment. It said something about how when a man loved his wife and held her tightly he passed his seed into her. Not having seen or heard anything about seed, I just assumed it was his pee. It was a couple of years later, when I was playing with myself in the bath and there was this sudden eruption, that I realised seed was something very different.

I made the mistake of mentioning this in class to my friend, Ian, who shared the same desk. He roared laughing but had the decency to put me on the right track. There was no pornography in those days, but somehow he had managed to get a copy of *Lady Chatterley's Lover*. It was out of this world. In those early days, I became very fond of myself. I tried to go to confession but it was a waste of time. I was genuinely worried that I would lose my soul. I had heard Dad talk passionately about a Jesuit priest, and when I heard that he had moved from Miltown to Rathfarnham, I decided that when I was on the annual school retreat I would call to see him.

I was confronted by a red-faced, jowly, plump priest, who ushered me into his room talking about how fond he was of Dad, how good he was organising the annual retreat for the architects, and how he knew my great uncle, Monsignor O'Reilly. So what could he do for me? I blurted out that I was having impure thoughts and doing impure things. His face got redder. He leaned towards me and told me that I was not to be worried. He looked at me. I was a little plump in those days and he asked if I played any sport. I told him I played rugby and he told me that if I played a bit more rugby I would be fine.

It was not long after that when my religious career with the Catholic Church came to an end. It was a quiet, personal affair. There was no public announcement, just a series of lies and deceptions, persuading Mum that I was going to Mass when, in reality, I went to a friend's house or, later, to the pub. But it was all too late. The Church had taken a firm grip of my body and soul. Even though I might have left the Church, it had not left me. No matter how much I tried to change, there were continual deep feelings of guilt, shame, awkwardness and embarrassment, not just about sex, but any form of desire or self-indulgence.

I can see myself, a small, docile, compliant boy, in my school uniform. Grandfather Muldoon would have been proud. The question is when, how and why I wanted to rebel against this cosy Catholic life. From a young age I seemed to question everything, never being satisfied with pat answers. I detested most of my school days. I was inspired by some of my teachers, but there was too much emphasis on discipline and control. Most of what remains of those days is a feeling of fear. We were beaten regularly, for small misdemeanours and minor mistakes. Often, the beatings were simply routine. You were asked a question, and if you got it wrong you had to leave your desk, and when the questioning was over, you lined up to be beaten. Some days the teachers were bored and they did not put much effort into the beatings: they might even yawn in between each one. Other days they were angry and they took it out on us.

Brother Thomas was the most cruel. He taught physics. Some days he would come in and be full of craic. But once a month, quite deliberately, he would have an inquest. We spent the first few minutes of each lesson trying to determine if it was to be a day of craic or pain. I was never any good at physics. Often the beatings were brutal and ritualistic. Most days, you might survive with a few belts of the leather. Other days you were told to leave the class. Outside you had to wait for Brother Jarlath. Before the end of each lesson, he stalked the corridors looking for boys who had been put out. You could hear him leave his office, and the thread of his footsteps on the tiled floor and his plodding up the stairs. As he approached, he would reach into his soutane, and like a cowboy, whip out his cane and walk up to you. There was no point in pleading. You just held out your hand. It was an automatic four. If he liked you, he went easy.

He did not like Michael Browne. He was a bit of a messer. One day, as we were parading our way through *Paradise Lost*, Jarlath burst in through the door and called Browne up the top of the class. He had just got a phone call from a mother whose daughter had been standing at a bus stop. She had her hand out to hail the bus. As Browne was cycling past, he seized the opportunity to spit a yellow gob into the palm of her hand. Jarlath was fuming. He was well over six feet tall and probably weighed fifteen stone, and he put all his weight and effort into giving Browne six of his best.

Of course, what happened to me and my friends was just a faint taste of what happened in primary and secondary schools in Ireland. I know now that while I was being beaten, boys of my own age were not just being beaten by religious brothers and priests but terrorised, brutalised and raped.

I often thought of driving down to Portlaise, where the elderly De La Salle brothers are brought to live out their final days, and asking to see Jarlath or Thomas, and spitting in their face. Uncle Oliver did manage to get as far as the front door of one of their houses and was all intent on boxing him on the nose, but was shocked into stillness by the sight of the small, bent figure that confronted him.

We were victims of victims, all part of a strange regime in which love and sexuality were deeply repressed, and where the innocent became scapegoats for anger and denial. There was one word which brothers and priests needed to scream out loud, one word that might have brought down their houses and schools of fear much earlier, a word that might have saved so many. But nobody could say it. Nobody could mention sex. I suspect that many brothers and priests were trapped in bad faith, ordinary decent men who were hoodwinked into believing they had a vocation, who ended up sacrificing their lives for a cause that many did not believe in. Sexually repressed men wrapped up in clerical dress. Maybe I should go to Portlaoise to forgive and forget, but I can't.

But there was a global tide sweeping across Ireland, and there was nothing much that brothers and priests could do to stop it. I never really liked or trusted the brothers, but soon, like many others, I began to despise and laugh at them. There was no fear, there was no respect.

It was a gentle rebellion. We did not do much other than laugh, disobey, listen to protest songs, and grow our hair long. We could see and hear the sixties from across the water in Britain. We headed there as soon and as often as we could. It was the promised land of freedom, pleasure, music, sex and drugs. But there was also a questioning of the older order, of the importance of family and the Catholic Church, of getting a good job, marrying and settling down. We did not want to put on the long cosy coat of middle-class values. It was about 'dropping out and turning on' but these were just catch-phrases for wearing jeans and long hair. It was also about going beyond the school curriculum. When I was in fifth class, I began to hang out with Tom Hobson. He became my best friend. He was reading different things. He introduced me to Beckett, Dylan Thomas, Salinger, Huxley and others. The burden of having to wear our Catholic overcoats was becoming intolerable. It was hard to breathe in that insufferable cultural air. We started a new conversation. We talked about our feelings, desires and hopes. We listened to pirate pop radio stations with our cheap Japanese transistors. We discovered Tamla Motown. We hung out in the Coffee Inn, the Zodiac, O'Shea's in Donnybrook. We swilled ideas around. The doors of perception of a new Ireland were opening slowly.

6

She never made it back down to the garden. I imagine her looking out the window, longing to be back down there, immersed in the smells and colours, delighting in the new growth, snarling and snatching at the intrusive weeds. Did she realise on that Monday morning that in a week's time she would be dead? Did I? The signs were everywhere. The daily visits of the hospice nurses; the heavy toll of the morphine; the pauses in her talk were increasing. She would drift in and out of conversation. Her fingers would freeze over the keys of her laptop. Her writing became more frail. She was having increasing difficulty getting up and down to the bathroom, and yet she carried on the daily routine, hoping the grim reaper would pass by her house.

Her sister, Maura, came to visit. I sat in the kitchen with her husband, Maxi. We talked about the possibility of putting in a temporary bath and toilet in the bedroom. It would be a major undertaking, there would be enormous disruption, and it would cost a lot. Was I in complete denial? Did she and I go on playing that game all week long, looking into the future, hoping? We were so good at delusion, until the day of the blood tests.

I had booked the ferry to go to France in the beginning of June, and so that afternoon we talked about how she could get there. Maybe she could fly and I would go on ahead with the car and the dog. She looked away from the window and into my eyes as if it was time for me to tell her the truth.

'My love, I don't think we will be going to France. You are not well enough.'

There was silence. I had thought of this and had an alternative on offer, a place where she had gone to as a child.

'Maybe we might go to Kelly's in Rosslare and get a room overlooking the sea.'

'Oh that would be wonderful. And can I swim in the sea?'

'Of course.'

It was the beginning of a long goodbye. I could not bear to think that she was going to go and that I would never see her again. I could go on pretending. She could go on pretending. We could reach out and touch reality now and again, but it was too frightening. Far better to pretend. She seemed to know I was the one who would collapse into tears, and so she steeled herself to play the game better than me. We were children again, playing a game. We always seemed to be playing games with each other from the very beginning: teasing, joking, cajoling, surprising, laughing.

I close my eyes and I can see her. Sometimes she is so real I think I must be dreaming. But I am wide awake. The past becomes a dream. I go back again, trying to grasp the space, the people, the moments in which we moved. What was I thinking? What did I say? What were my feelings and emotions? The past is all there is left of her. We shared a brief trajectory through time.

Stella House was once the most popular dancehall in south Dublin. I had started going there when I was fifteen. During the day it was a plain old hall, but with music, lighting and luscious young girls it became a place of erotic dreams, full of suburban promise.

Going to Stella on a Saturday night was an equal and opposite reaction to going to church on Sunday. I had given up on saving my soul. I was there to unleash my body. Here there was real hope of being saved. Every time I stepped into Stella, I lived in hope. She would come to me, she would choose me, whoever she was. She would be beautiful. We would fall madly in love. She would give me everything I wanted. She would be the perfect woman: Brigitte Bardot made flesh.

Even when she did not turn up, there was still hope of some brief tryst, of arousal, a French kiss and, maybe, even better, the feel of a soft breast. The close dances were best. These were the essence of fornication and concupiscence about which the priests had warned me so often.

Just to be able to hold the body of a girl up against me, to move in unison to the music, to feel her hair, to look into her face, to kiss her lips, to let my tongue slide into her soft, welcoming mouth.

We were young, unregulated, gyrating bodies. There were no rules to the dancing, and yet everyone knew what was permissible, what was risky, and what was out of order. There were things that could be said and done; moves that could be made. It was a subtle game. It could be emotionally devastating. I learnt how to hold a body, when to move back for a potential kiss, how daring to be with my tongue, how much I could move my hand up and down. Close dancing was having sex by other means. It was a full body encounter, often with loss of semen. And then there was the ignominy of standing in the toilet, with a small map of Greenland just below my trouser pocket.

It was the end of the Easter Holidays in 1969. I was due to return to my teaching job in Saint Omer in the north of France. I had been there since the beginning of the year. I was forlorn. I was not very happy. It was a boarding school run by the De La Salle brothers. I had hated most of my schooldays in Dublin. I had meticulously planned my run away from home after finishing school in June 1968. I had hoped to get to North Africa. I have no idea why. I flew to Madrid and, after a fruitless month trying to find work – it did not help that I did not have a word of Spanish – I turned myself in at a monastery. From there I was sent to a family in Cuidad Real, supposedly to teach English to one of their many children, but in reality I was adopted for two months. I came home in November and went to France the following January.

It was the Saturday after Easter. Rory Gallgher and Taste were playing. I had paid too much attention to the music. Now it was the last set. I was frustrated and annoyed. Yet again I did the tour, up and around the outskirts of the dance floor, in between the pillars. I was a no-hoper on my way to becoming an early-leaver. On the dance floor, those who were lucky enough to have something to hang on to were holding on tight. I was two-thirds up the south-side. I passed her by and got a glimpse. She was standing with her back leaning against the pillar. She seemed to have appeared from nowhere. What a glorious prospect. But the signals were mixed. She was slouching against a pillar with a look of disdain and disinterest. In the instant of this look and assessment, I decided to give her a miss. It was too late in the night to suffer rejection. She was too good-looking to be out there on her own. Something must have happened: waiting for the boyfriend to return from the toilet, maybe they'd had a row. No point in making an approach. No point in being refused and turning feelings of loneliness and despair into ones of hurt and anger.

But as I walked on, I looked back, another quick glimpse. This time I was sure there was a smile, quick and faint. Was I making it up? Was this a fantasy? I had reached the next pillar. And then, as if she had lassoed me with her thoughts, I was turning back and walking up to her. I said nothing. I motioned to the dance floor. We entered the crowd and moved our bodies about in an appropriate manner. There was going to be no slow dance.

And then it was all over, the dance, the set, the evening. We stopped. We looked into each other's eyes. Her face was wrapped in soft, creamy skin. Her auburn hair drooped down over her forehead, partly covering her cheeks. But what attracted me most were her eyes. As I gazed into them, I was mesmerised. They were deep, green pools. I was drowning in them.

There was no sense of sex. I did not feel aroused. There was instead a sense of awe. I grappled for something to say. I wanted to be cool. I wanted to say something different. What possible line could I come out with that hadn't been said thousands of times before? I was struggling. In desperation I almost gave up. She was waiting patiently. I continued to look into her eyes. She did not blink.

'Woof,' I said.

There was a short delay. She held me waiting. She didn't take her eyes off me. It was only a couple of seconds, but it was the defining moment in my life.

'Meow,' she replied.

She smiled, a full, warm, inviting smile. Her mouth opened up. Her sparkling white teeth shone in the purple disco light. She laughed. I knew I was in with a chance. But I had to make my pitch quickly. People were beginning to leave. Briefly I told her my story, that I was returning to France the following Tuesday. I asked if I could see her the next day, Sunday. She did not hesitate. She did not play the game of being hard to get. She just said yes and gave me her phone number.

I love the arbitrariness of it all. Such a tiny incident turned my life down a completely different track. Another second later she might have moved or looked the other way. Life is a beautiful chaos. If the meteor that destroyed the dinosaurs had been eight minutes late, they might have survived and humans may never have evolved. In the infinity of time, in the history of human being, this one small encounter was meaningless, and yet, in the history of my life, in the history of understanding what it is to be human, it was all that life is about.

And what if I could have used a remote control and fast forwarded to me now, lying in our bed without her, unable to move, stricken with grief. Would I have changed my mind? Would I have done anything different?

I like to think that our meeting was pure chance, Cupid firing his arrow. In reality it was very predictable. I can see myself caught in time and space. We were just two suburban middle-class Dublin kids; débutantes coming out into Western culture in the 1960s. It was so intensely personal, and yet it was so social. We were both acting out our roles. Our thoughts, words and body movements were parts of a cultural script that was emerging in Ireland at the time. We were playing a game of romantic love. We were being coy and erotic. What we thought was personal was shaped by global media messages flowing in through the airwaves. We were part of a soft sexual revolution.

I was awake and in love from an early hour on that Sunday, wondering when it would be best to phone. What if she rebuked me and told me to look her up when I got back from France? Maybe her coming on to me was a play of my imagination. But when I did phone, she was effusive. She gave me directions to her house. I would walk down to Dundrum, up the hill towards Sandyford and, after I passed the Pallottine Fathers' house on the right, there would be a road into a housing estate. Bally Olaf was three exits up from this.

A long driveway led to a modern two-storey flat-roofed white house with pale blue metal window frames. It was set in a large garden surrounded by tall fir trees. There were large greenhouses on both sides of the driveway. I knew from my father that the greenhouse area to the left had once been a mink farm. I was walking into warm, comfortable wealth.

She answered the door. The house was full of noisy activity. She had three sisters and two brothers, all around the same age. She did not like all the attention that we were getting, so she brought me up to her bedroom. She had no sense of shame. I felt awkward, but I was as excited as a dog who had been shown a lead. I had no idea what was coming next. It was ludicrous to think that we were going to go up to her bedroom and have sex while her family romped around downstairs. I was imagining all sorts of things.

The scene in the bedroom was far from a still life: it was a kaleidoscopic mess. It was as if she was trying to create a Francis Bacon studio in her bedroom. There were posters on the wall, clothes and school books everywhere. The clothes were all bright colours with bold designs: dresses, skirts and tops that she had made herself. There was no apology for the place being in such a mess. She was showing off, delighted with herself and her room. It was as if I had been invited to a private exhibition of herself and her work. She had obviously been given free rein with the space. The walls were painted roughly in pink. They were offset in the corner by the wash-basin which she had tried to paint red, but which was peeling away like skin from an Irish sunbather.

And there was music. She had brought up the small record player from downstairs. At home, we still had to make do with the crackling sounds that came from a small Japanese yellow transistor radio. She put on the Beatles' *White Album*. I did not know it existed. She sang and moved around the room, singing along with ease to Rocky Racoon. She was putting on a private show for me, and yet there seemed to be little self-consciousness. She was a happy, natural born middle-class girl. I was ecstatic. All my Sundays were coming together and I had to leave the following Tuesday.

She was demure and mischievous. She smiled. She took my hand. 'Where are we going?' 'For a walk,' she said. Was this another chance to lead me astray? She was being deliberately coquettish and alluring, humming a song as she danced along down the driveway, and out into the fields. She was play acting at being young, romantic and in love. The more she played it the more she felt it was real. I was her new boy. She was having her way with me.

There were two fields behind the house. We climbed through the fence and walked up into the second field. It was a sunny Sunday. From the top of the field we looked back down to the house. Imagine living in the suburbs of Dublin with a big modern house, huge gardens and greenhouses, and then fields. I was overwhelmed by the grandeur and wealth. There were some cattle that stood idly by. When we turned the corner where the gorse bushes were beginning to blush yellow, she stopped. We were no longer in view of the house. She did not wait long. She smiled. She parted her hair and leaned forward. I could kiss her now.

She had practised kissing by imagining the scene and the moves she would make with her tongue and lips. In those days, the big thing was whether a girl would be bold enough not just to receive the boy's tongue into her mouth, but to go on to push her tongue into his. The boldest girls would harden their tongue before entering the boy's mouth as if they were taking on the role of being the penetrating male.

For all her imagination and practice, the kissing did not last long. But it was more than just a peck. It was a sign of approval. We turned and faced into the cattle who had moseyed over to have a look. She acted the confident cowgirl and whooshed them away.

We walked back down the field and entered the wood, their own private wood. It was full of exotic trees and plants, with walls and water features. It had once been a landscaped garden, part of the Balally estate, but it had become a complete wilderness over the previous fifty years. We came across her father aimlessly clearing the path from brambles. He was smoking a cheroot as he hacked away. I introduced myself. He stopped and looked at me carefully.

'Are you any relation to Jack Inglis?' he asked.

'He's my uncle,' I said.

He smiled and looked at me.

'Jack hits a lovely long drive,' he said. 'Straight down the middle. Low along the ground at first, but then it rises up like a white star soaring high into the distance.'

I had been given a south Dublin middle-class blessing. Being in the same golf club would have been good enough, but to have an uncle who was admired was an added bonus.

The next day Aileen visited Ardtona. This house visiting was unusual. Mostly new emerging couples like ourselves would have stayed clear of formal house visits and hung out in free houses, dances and whatever pubs we could get into. But she and I were caught in a whirlwind. I wanted to open up to her as much as I could in the time we had left. I wanted her to see inside my life, to see the aristocratic space in which I grew up, to meet my family. I wanted to impress her.

She came up the granite steps, in through the big white hall door surrounded by stained glass, and stepped into the long wood-panelled hall. I took her coat. I suggested a walk in the garden and slowly took her down through the hall, past the grandfather clock, the old oil portrait in the back-hall, out the back door and down the steps, through the fir trees and into the garden. It was still an enchanting place, full of paths bordered by box hedges that wandered around a large lawn surrounded by apple and pear trees. We turned left, down past the flower bed where the asters and lupins grew. The crab apple tree was coming into bloom. The path weaved around down to the back of the garden, past the dishevelled greenhouse where Dad had once grown grapes and tomatoes. Then it turned right, up along the far side of the lawn where there was a tall privet hedge. We stopped and kissed under the metal arch wrapped with wisteria. We walked on up past the rhododendrons and raspberry plants, past the vegetable plot and on to the side gate before turning right along the wire fence that held the loganberries. The garden was like an aged aunt who, despite the ravages of time, managed to reveal glimpses of her former beauty.

We went inside and sat on the couch in the living room. Mum came back from her afternoon trip to the shops. I thought that she was warm and welcoming, but Aileen did not see past the Victorian lady. Her first impression was that Mum was rather cold and formal. Maybe it was that while her Mum was a country girl who had become middle class, my Mum had taken on the formal body, airs and graces of her father and mother.

She invited Aileen to stay to tea. She could not refuse but she was nervous, intimidated by the grandeur of the dining room, the mahogany table and chandelier, the marble fireplace and the grand piano in the corner. She felt she was being scrutinised and that her manners would let her down. We were both from the same class, but there were important fine differences. Aileen was a part of the new upper middle class, with a lot more wealth. I came from an established professional middle class with titles and positions.

She came to see me off at the boat in Dun Laoghaire the following evening. I was going back to the fields of northern France, back to my small room in the dormitory with the senior pupils. I was spellbound and distraught. I was eighteen, she was sixteen. We promised to write, and I did the day I arrived back in France.

> *God I miss you. You said that although we may write we will forget each other. I will never forget you, and I never want to... To be oneself, like you are, is an achievement which thousands wish to achieve and fail miserably. It comes naturally to you, and I hope will always remain that way.*

She replied:

Tom it's not fair for you if I write I love you when I don't really know you. Oh, I know I like you so very very much; maybe I'm just scared to say I love you. Oh, help Tom, I don't know. Isn't it so beautiful to know when you love, you are loving with love on loan from God. Tom you know I love God, believe in God. It's amazing I suppose that I can believe in God so much and yet find Christian Doctrine class the most boring half-hour of the day.

God was everywhere in those days. He was part of who we were, the way we knew and understood ourselves and the world in which we lived. Even though he was on the way out, he still lay across our hearts, minds and bodies. We were caught in the middle of a long process of social change. Young couples like Aileen and I, practising at being romantic, had moved from formal courting to informal dating. The sixties were about expunging the past from our systems. We thought we were cool, devising a new way of talking, being and hanging out. We were cast into the age-old role of writing love letters, trying to describe our feelings and emotions, sharing our fears and anxieties. But our mindsets – the words we wrote, the ideas we had, the spaces we lived in – were still all very Catholic. Her last letter that Spring was written while she was on school retreat.

And the sun is playing on the water, and the nib of my pen. There are so many insects here, I suppose because of the trees, I'm just thinking would there be as many insects as miles to the nearest star. The stream is dancing down from one rock to the next. It's making a gigantic noise, maybe you're supposed to have quiet to think. You just can't have quiet here; a bell's gone; someone's just trampled down the grass and made a path; no the winds... Tom I'm sorry the last letter was so long in getting to you but don't ever be worried or imagine that I love you less than I say. Far as I do know there couldn't be anyone else but you. Tom you know I'm waiting for you, but don't ever be scared if your feelings change. Oh how I miss you so much, Tom it will be so good won't it. You told me about you, and I like you so much. When you're laughing and feeling happy, I want to be happy too and when you are sad and down I want to listen and tell you not to worry. I want to be with you now, now is here and it's life and it's missing you. Tom will you love that I care for you.

Towards the end of May, she had stopped writing. I was distraught. I wrote to her:

If only you would tell me exactly how you feel then I would know, but otherwise I live in a state of uncertainty, imagining.

Then I switched to being detached, and tried to develop an objective understanding of what was happening to me:

Human relations are impossible to understand, for if a man's mind is almost impossible to conceive and understand, how possibly can we understand the relation between two separate different and unlike minds. Thus love is impossible to understand and yet its consequences can be enormous. Few philosophers have discussed the power of love because it varies according to each person, but it is one of the most dominating factors of our lives.

That summer, I went to work in a pea factory in Lowestoft, East Anglia. I was on the lookout for love and sex. But while Terry Corboy, Des Cannon, myself and the rest of us Irish lads were keen to score, we were completely at sea in the art of romance. We spent far too much time in our own company, drinking ourselves silly. There was very little attempt to engage with the local girls. We were like millions before us: a migrant community of Irish workers who did not fit in with the locals. Bar the attraction of tits and ass, there was little we saw in the local English lassies, and there was little that they saw in us.

I arrived back in Dublin in early September. Aileen was very much on my mind, but I did not have the courage to phone her. The first Saturday, I went into Kehoe's in South Anne Street, which had become one of my favourite haunts. It was still early. There were a couple of soul mates, but I was too distracted with thoughts of Aileen. I took the plunge, and walked up to the phone boxes at the top of Grafton Street. Her younger sister, Trish, answered the phone. When she said who it was, Aileen told her to tell me that she was not there. Trish refused, and I found out later that she said that Aileen should talk to me, that I sounded lovely. Aileen relented. I asked her to come into town to meet me. No, she said she was doing something else. Would she come to the party in Niamh Coffee's in Cowper Road? Doubtful. I decided that she was giving me the cold shoulder, my attempt to renew the relationship had failed, and whatever it was I thought we had, was over. I was dejected. I returned to the pub. Friends came in, we shared our summer experiences, but I made no mention of Aileen. It was a male culture: to talk about my feelings and emotions would have been out of place. So I did the usual Irish thing: I sublimated my sense of loss in pints of stout and headed out to the party.

There was a good buzz, but I was sinking into despair. All the activity was out in the back so I slipped away to the living room and found an armchair into which I collapsed. Meanwhile, Aileen had changed her mind. She persuaded her friend, Margo, and her boyfriend, Charlie, to drive her out to the party. While they waited in the car she went in and mingled through the partygoers but she could not find me. She was told that I must have gone home. She was about to leave when she looked into the drawing room. She saw me. I have no idea how long I was there. She shook me awake. I was dazed, confused and drunk. She was furious. She stormed out of the house. I managed to get to her before she got into the car. I pleaded my case. She relented and agreed that I could phone her the next day. I did and we were back together.

7

Death eats away at meaning. It makes life seem ludicrous. Five days before she died, I was sitting in my chair beside our bed. It was hard to concentrate. Every minute or so I would look over at her. She was sitting up with the newspaper. She had her glasses on. She looked really well. She was concentrating, trying to do the crossword. It was a ritual we had developed over the previous year, a way of doing something together. She had slowed down so much. The doses of morphine were strong. While she could read the clue, even if she got the answer, putting the letters into the boxes was a real struggle. I could see the effort, the determination. I could have offered to take over, but that would have been giving in. Instead, she struggled on. Being able to do the crossword was another sign that she was not dying. I could see the resolve on her face. It was as if she was a young child, colouring in the outline of a house, desperately trying to keep within the lines.

'Timely money in eight, something, something, r,' she said.

I got it quickly but I had to wait. I could not snap out the answer. I had to give her a chance.

'Salaries,' I suggested.

'No, it doesn't fit.'

And she drifted off with the morphine and I waited for her to come back.

'Currency.'

'Yes, that's it.'

She filled in the letters.

'Did you read that article in the paper about the euro?' she asked.

'No.'

'It must be the worst designed currency in the world. They had so much time and money to get it right and they got it so wrong. I still cannot tell the difference between a twenty and fifty cent piece.'

She was not just miffed or upset, she was angry and frustrated. I started to panic. I wondered if she might want to try to do something about it. Write a letter to the paper. A parting shot from a dying artist. Surely there were other things to get annoyed about? The arbitrariness of life, the inequity of death. Maybe the euro was a scapegoat, a metaphor for not being able to do anything about herself.

What do you do when you on the verge of entering the dark abyss? Do you talk about death, or do you just keep on talking as you have always done about the mundane things of life, the need to get the curtains cleaned, to cancel the plumber, to get some more paper napkins.

'Tom, that reminds me, I must go through the bank accounts with you.'

It was all becoming a bit too much. What a way to spend the days before you die, pouring over bank statements. I smiled and lied.

'Not now my love, maybe some other time.'

In our early days of courting, we used to meet in Stephen's Green and sit under a tree by the lake. If it was raining, we went into the pagoda. I was in first year Social Science in UCD. It was the autumn of 1969. Aileen was in her final year in school. She was seventeen. She would come directly from school. I was on a high, but I was uneasy. I was dazzled by her confidence. She was not afflicted by doubt, shame or remorse. She was intoxicated by life, exhilarated by the possibilities of what we might do together. There was no angst, anger or resentment. I was full of contradictions. I wanted to be a part of this whirlwind. She wanted me to sing and dance with her in the pagoda, but I was paralysed with embarrassment. What if one of the lads saw me with this schoolgirl in her uniform? I wanted to show her off. I wanted her to be in one of her snazzy, fashionable trouser suits. I wanted to parade her down Grafton Street. Most of all, I wanted to bring her into the pubs where I hung out with my friends. But women and pubs in the 1960s were immiscible.

Pubs were male havens where barmen dispensed the milk of human kindness, mostly to men, usually in the form of black pints of stout and glasses of golden whiskey. They had a structure and logic that everyone embodied from an early age. Pubs were divided into three parts: the main bar, the lounge and the snug. The latter was for women. The lounge was where a man might bring a woman. The bar was strictly an all-male zone. Bars could be loud and lewd. They were places where men could be uncivilised but in a controlled manner. There were signs warning people not to sing, but regulars were not deterred. There was sawdust on the floor, to collect spits and splashes from glasses and stomachs. The toilets were close to running sewers. Regularly, towards the end of the evening, the toilet floor would be awash with piss. To attempt a crap was a real adventure. There was never any toilet paper. There was never any hot water. There was never any means of drying your hands.

Since everyone wanted to be accepted into pubs, it was a sellers' market. There was always a surfeit of customers. Barmen presided behind the counter like policemen. It was essential to be deferential. They had to be cajoled. They were the gatekeepers to pleasure and had to be approached with caution. One wrong look, one hint of an incorrect attitude, and you might not be served. Regulars were often barred, sometimes for a week or more, sometimes for life. If you were barred, you had to try to persuade your friends to come out in sympathy with you. But most men were devoted to their local pub. So, if you were barred, the only other solution was to go back in, sober and quietly, preferably in the morning when nobody else was around and, while not exactly apologising (that would be too great a dishonour), to act in a suitably meek and mild manner.

Young drinkers like me had to serve our time as customers. I was three years into my apprenticeship. I was learning how to deal with barmen. Women in pubs were about as welcome as Muslims in a synagogue. They had to be quiet and modest. They could speak, but only when they were spoken to. They were expected to nurse their drinks, to sip their sherries, ports, babychams or half-pints of beer, but no pints. The worst thing for any woman was to behave like a man, to drink too much and get drunk. Women were persuaded, and many actually believed themselves, that drink was like sex: it was something in which only men took pleasure. Aileen was not that easily persuaded.

Sinnotts was just off Stephen's Green. It had a magnificent, high, ornate ceiling with intricate, coloured plasterwork, enormous chandeliers and a long, marble counter that ran the length of the pub. It was popular with bankers and businessmen. Some of us young men took to going there on a Wednesday afternoon. I suggested to Aileen that she might come in and join us. I was a bit nervous. I was not sure how the lads or the barmen would take to her. It was a brave move, but I felt confident that she would pull it off.

There was a group of four or five of us sitting at one of the tables half way down the bar. I had my eye on the front door, waiting for her to come in. We were laughing and joking. And then I saw what I didn't want to see. Aileen came striding into the bar as if she was John Wayne looking for an outlaw. She was dressed in her green school uniform. I went still and silent. My friends looked round to see what I was seeing. She strolled up to me. She was smiling as if nothing was wrong. I looked away and put my head down and mumbled.

'Lads, this is Aileen.'

'Hi guys.'

I was frantically trying to think of some way out of this.

'I was just about to go.'

'But you have a lot left in your pint.'

'Oh, I'll finish it quickly.'

She was reading me.

'So are you not going to buy me a drink?' she asked.

'I'm not too sure they will serve you.'

The lads were silent. She looked at me scornfully and then at them. It was the look of a none too happy reverend mother disappointed with her pupils. Nobody was jumping up to be the gallant knight in shining armour. She turned around and went up to the barman and, looking him in the eye, asked for a small Jameson whiskey. He did not hesitate. He picked out a glass, took out the small measure, and served it to her. She came back to the table. Her mood had changed; now she was defiant. I was mortified. I mumbled that she could not do this as she could get us all barred. She stared at me aghast. She got up abruptly, and without saying a word walked towards the door. She had not touched her drink.

I went after her. She was in floods of tears outside. It had been an enormous challenge for her, one to which she had been building up all afternoon, and I had completely failed her. I apologised profusely, pleading with her to return. She refused. She was going home. I was caught in no-man's land. Should I go back into my friends and try to regain my honour and let her go alone back across Stephen's Green, remorseful and tearful? And so on South King street on that autumnal afternoon, I was catapulted into a decision. I left my pint and the lads and walked her to her bus stop.

Aileen was a novice, learning how to operate in male spaces, refusing to be put down. She knew there was a proper time and place for women and a proper way for them to behave, but she was willing to challenge these notions. It was a mixture of pure self-confidence and naivety. A small cultural battle took place in Sinnotts that afternoon. There was a lot of honour and pride at stake.

Aileen mixed her brazenness with charm. She had a way of smiling that held you in her green eyes. And while you were dazzled, she began to engage with you, smiling, laughing, touching, all the time holding you with her eyes. She was a flirt. Throughout the seventies, she became a regular in Kehoe's. By this stage, women were allowed in the main bar. Andy, the grumpy old head barman, had given way to Nicky, who was efficient and genial, and who developed a soft spot for her and she for him.

Those moments of entering Kehoe's seem eternal. It was another world, a cocoon of comfort and consolation, where everything was the same but anything was possible, where ideas were swilled around with pints as we thrashed out the meaning of life. It was a heady mixture of exuberance and idealism. And it had its own little rituals. Walking in through the saloon doors, we would go straight to the counter, sit down and wait to be greeted by Nicky. He would come by with his smile, wipe down the counter, and look across to her. The wiping would stop and there were the usual opening exchanges. Nicky was slow and urbane. He had the politeness never to stay too long.

Aileen saw Kehoe's as a fashion parade. She had become very skilled at making the most of scant resources, getting dress patterns in Switzer's, buying remnants in Hickeys, and coming up with brightly coloured flamboyant dresses and skirts. She loved the swirl of a full dress. She matched these with sparkling necklaces and long, dangling earrings. The stage was set, the old wooden interior, the nicotine stained walls and ceilings, the fog of smoke, the smell of stale beer, the sounds of laughter, the glances of the customers. It was show time.

There were very few dandies left in Dublin in the 1970s, but if we got into Kehoe's by seven on a Saturday, we managed to meet one. He dressed impeccably, always wore a rose in his buttonhole, carried a cane, and drank snipes of champagne. It was his treat after work: he owned a jewellery shop on Anne Street. He ignored me completely as if I was some courier who had delivered him a bunch of flowers. But he always looked Aileen over, admired her clothes, asked and made comments about her jewellery. He would drink her in. She would lick up to him.

'What a lovely dress, I really like the flow of colour. Did you make it yourself?'

'You are such a charmer.'

'Now, my beautiful young lady, you must join me in some champagne.'

He would call Nicky over.

'Another snipe and another glass please Nicky.'

Aileen revelled in the exotic dance that took place between them. They were two professional flirts thrown into the ring together. Aileen smiled and laughed. She would lean over and push him away. He would lean in and take her hand and kiss it.

The gang, mostly students, who began to congregate in Kehoe's were a mixture of posers and counter-culture activists. The swinging 60s arrived late in Ireland, but it did have an impact on those of us who finished school in 1968. I had seen the remnants of the student revolts in France, and earlier in Spain. In Kehoe's, there were aspiring philosophers, novelists, poets and film-makers mixed in with rising alcoholics and drug-addicts. Most of us were students. It was a strange elite. We were young, cultural critics trying to be sophisticated cosmopolitans. The dress code for men was a university scarf and book. Some people went as far as to have a copy of Mao's *Little Red Book.* I preferred Marcuse's *One Dimensional Man.* What bound the gang together was a strong resistance to orthodox Catholic culture, the dull arm of what was generally labelled 'the system'. There was a feeling that we had been colonised, brainwashed into becoming staid, respectable, middle-class members of society. We had to rebel.

Inevitably, much of this was expressed in smoking dope. It was not just a pleasure, it was a badge. Our counter-culture world was divided into 'heads' and 'straights'. Straights were to be avoided, especially when you were stoned. They were the staid conservatives who had sold their souls to family, church and nation. They refused to think outside the box. Us heads were bound by a common belief and practice: we saw and understood the world differently.

Some 'heads' were more like hippies than others, but we were all united by the task of going out into the usual haunts, foraging for some dope, then at the end of the night gathering into small bedsits, methodically rolling joints and passing them round as if they were some sacred host. It was a ritual ceremony full of pomp and glory, full of its own strange rules. We listened to music, we drank and we sang. It was not political. Ours was a new and better way of being religious. We were ecstatic. We cast aside the fear of death, and embraced pleasure. We were the new hedonists.

We wanted to eliminate the taken-for-granted Catholic way of being. We wanted to embrace the outside world. Little we saw in *gaelic* culture that was ours. We were mostly apolitical. Very few were members of political parties. I toyed with anarchism, others were vague Trots and Stickies. There were no Provos. Most of us seemed to be more concerned about the Greek generals and apartheid than about what was going on in Northern Ireland.

The only thing that bound us males together, other than dope, was rugby. We had all gone to Catholic rugby playing schools, which was part of a quintessential Dublin middle-class upbringing. While most had managed to expunge the Church from our sense of self, it was a different matter when it came to rugby. It had become embodied as part of who we were. No amount of dope would make it go away.

I was never that bothered about rugby, but I did not want to be left out of the pack. I was someone who believed but did not practice. Playing rugby was seen as a serious, if not sacred, matter. It was a weird mixture, when 'heads' became 'straights' – and most rugby players were very straight. One evening I got chased out of the showers for declaring that the only reason I played rugby was to be able to share the shower afterwards.

Even though it was the sixties, the threat of homosexuality was enormous. Throwing a gay spanner into the showers fucked up the all male, macho group. Like many other things in my voyage of self-discovery, I took gayness to the limit, testing the edge beyond which my rugby friends could not go. Yes, it was fine to tell queer jokes, to go into Bartley Dunne's – the only gay pub in Dublin at the time – and look into their world and pretend to be gay. It was something else to explore homosexual feelings and emotions, to open the homoerotic box. It was beyond the realm of accepted thought, let alone behaviour.

Aileen had no time for rugby. She refused to come and watch me play. It was not so much standing on the sideline in the wind and rain at a desolate pitch in the back of beyond, it was more the repartee in the pub after matches, with the male kings performing for each other and their adoring queens. Rugby songs and crude jokes were not for her. She hated conventions, particularly those which said what women could and could not do. She drank whiskey as an act of rebellion. She disliked that bikes were always black, so she painted hers green. She got tired of cycling up and down from Bally Olaf to Ardtona, so she got herself a small motorcycle. Aileen was not so much a feminist as an artist. She was an excited young woman who wanted to explore the world, imaginatively, visually and physically. Watching men running around a field after a ball, and then go to the pub and drink themselves silly, did very little for her.

We were becoming close. We learnt to talk, going back over and over events to discover what it was that caused one of us to feel hurt, dismayed, angered, frustrated or annoyed. We were two emotional volcanoes of self exploding together, each sparked on by the other.

But if I draw back out from the rugby, from Kehoe's and the headiness of love, romance, sex and dope, I can see how we were bodies and souls caught in time, who believed passionately that we were driving the car of history but, realistically, it was being driven by forces and processes of change way beyond us. We were being carried along a flow of change that was sweeping over Dublin from all over the world. We began to exude a warm glow. We became confident of our love for each other. We may have been young romantics playing roles devised by others, but it was rich and thick. We were the young cats that got the cream.

I can smell her. I can hear her sleeping. I can feel my hand drifting down to her thigh. I can feel her warm body, her soft skin and my excitement as she responds positively, yawning and stretching to the delight of being awake, of feeling aroused. Caresses mixed with purrs. I have no urgent desire, just a feeling of physical delight, letting go, holding her close. In those moments I achieved transcendence. It took years to get it right, to perfect the pleasure, to know when and how to linger, to wait for her.

When we first started dating, I had no idea how to make love, be romantic or have good sex. I had no idea how to chat up a girl the right way, how to sweet talk her. The best model, and the one I most admired, was Sean Connery as James Bond. Women fell for him like apples from a tree. He would just look at them, make some sexy comment, and they would have their clothes off and be in bed with him within seconds. The real world was a bit different.

In the summer of 1969, I went straight from teaching in France to canning peas in Lowestoft in East

Anglia. Although she had stopped writing to me, Aileen presided in her absence. When the pea season ended, I got a job on a farm in Norfolk where they sterilised daffodil bulbs. The farm also contained a Concordia camp to which young people came from all over the world. It was there that I met Janice. She was a direct, American girl who spoke animatedly and at great length about Gurdjieff, the mystic philosopher. It was all very mystical and spiritual. I was trying to get my mind around the notion of how we were all interconnected elements within the universe and, at the same time, trying to get my hands on her.

For the first few times we met, we sat and talked. But things changed. I agreed with her suggestion that we should go for a walk together, so she came to collect me late during the following afternoon, in the barn where we sterilised the bulbs. I had to do some work and went out the back to check on something and when I came back in she had taken off her top. 'Let's skip the walk,' she said. She opened up her arms and I fell straight into her large breasts. I could not believe my luck. There was to be no awkward fumbling, no fears or hesitations. The message was clear: here you are kiddo, come and get it.

I thought of Bond, said the right things, caressed, stroked, and held myself back. I thought I was doing well, and was moving in for the ultimate prize when she stopped and sat upright. I was sure that I had done something wrong, that she was unsatisfied with my moves and the way I was handling matters. But no, she told me quite calmly that she had had gonorrhoea, that she had gone to the doctor, taken the antibiotics, and was sure she was okay again. I shrivelled. I had heard stories about 'the clap', mythical urban stories about willies falling off or becoming sterile for ever more. There was an eruption of emotions. I was petrified, but I was also still excited. Here it was on offer, a dream come true, and suddenly everything was turned upside down. I was on the verge of life fulfilment, and it was as if death had popped its head in the door and told me not to be worried that he would wait for me outside.

As she sat there calmly, waiting for a response, I started to shake. Had I already become contaminated? How does this thing spread? Was Janice really a prostitute masquerading as an ordinary decent American student? What should I do? What could I do? This had never happened to Bond. I tried to be polite, but actions speak louder than words, and soon I was up on my feet and walking away, leaving Janice in tears.

I was naïve and innocent about sex, love and romance. I had no idea what to do or say when I began courting Aileen. Even though she was younger, she seemed so much more skilled in these matters. At least she had some exposure to the discourse if not the practice: she had read magazines like *Jackie*, which were full of stories and advice about love. For me it was like learning a new game, how to be aware, sensitive, caring: how to talk openly and honestly about myself, my feelings and experiences. But what was amazing for me was listening to Aileen talk so much about herself, revealing her passions, fears, hopes, desires, disappointments. As much as I had never learnt to touch and caress, I had never learnt to talk about myself. There had been nothing even close to this language in my life before. It was easy to become addicted. I did not realise how dependent I was becoming on being with her, continually talking, listening and bonding.

Yes, I had learnt to talk about myself with my friend, Tom. We had explored sensual pleasure and gone beyond many boundaries in our conversations. But with Aileen, I was willing and able to put myself on the line with a woman without any fear of shame or embarrassment. I began to express myself physically and emotionally. It was as if I never played golf before and soon I was hitting long drives straight down the middle. The years of sexual repression into which I had been born, which had been deeply inculcated by my parents and the De La Salle brothers, were cast off like old skin. I was with this warm, loving woman who showed me how to play without fear of losing, who encouraged me to make new moves, who took my hand and led me dancing through fields of love and sex.

When Aileen and I started fondling and stroking each other, my main concern was my own pleasure. My greatest fear was coming too soon and ending up with Greenland over my clothes. I had very little knowledge of her body, knowing only that she had what I needed, breasts and a vagina. I had no idea that women took pleasure in sex. I had no idea that she had a clitoris, that she had orgasms and that there were ways of pleasuring her. I did not reflect on it much, but if I had, I was probably convinced that she got pleasure from giving me pleasure and that if I did not come, or came too soon, it was deeply frustrating and disappointing for her.

Aileen was a calm and patient teacher. She took my fingers and showed me how to arouse her, to feel her clitoris in a way that it became moist, when and how to penetrate her without hurting. It was an education, learning how to fulfil her fantasies and desires. I learned how to use words and phrases, to emit sounds, to talk passionately and erotically. It was a whole new language, a whole new practice. It was the beginning of physically realising myself through her.

In the early days, after we got back together in the autumn of '69, we visited each other in our homes. In Ardtona, we would withdraw to thc study. Aileen would arrive down on her little motorcycle and we would sit on the couch listening to records. The previous summer my brother, Maurice, had bought a record player, and so Aileen and I were able to listen to my collection of three albums from Taste, Led Zepplin and Ten Years After that I had bought with my earnings at the end of the summer . But they were not good for making love, so I bought Leonard Cohen and Tim Hardin. We kissed, cuddled and fondled. We never went all the way on the study couch, but we came close. There was too much risk: the polite knock on the door and the intrusive entrance of Mum, Dad, Maurice or Judy.

And then it came to fruition. We were alone in the living room in Bally Olaf. We started fondling. It became more erotic and lustful. I wanted to go all the way, but I did not want to hurt her. We put the cushions from the couch on the floor. She was committed, but uncertain. We were not married. We had no condoms. If she became pregnant there would be hell to pay.

Could she trust me? Would I stand by her? I had no money or prospects. But lust is a wonderful thing. It has its own logic. I was on the verge of transcendence. Aileen was excited but there was a physicality to making love that she had not expected. We were both virgins. Aileen was also a bit scared. I tried to reassure her. I kept looking into her eyes and telling her how much I loved her. I felt myself coming. I withdrew. I came. It was beautiful and awkward. We held each other tightly. We did not talk. We just sat on the couch, holding on to each other for dear life. She was sore and frightened. I kept reassuring her.

And so, as it was in the end, so it was at the beginning. There is something spiritual and eternal in those moments of pure bodily being, something intensely personal, beyond words, a place where God and the devil reign supreme.

I try to go back to that moment on the floor, to relive and feel those beautiful, stupid, fumbling movements. I can see us lying there, writhing, clothes half on and off caught in the middle of time, in the middle of making love. I can see two young people engrossed in life, oblivious of death.

Did I give a damn? Although I genuinely cared for and loved Aileen, I also wanted to have sex. There was something animalistic going on. I was driven, but wanted to be sensitive and caring. I had a longing to fuck, but I also had a longing to love. I was all over the place. I was wrapped up in sex, passion, intimacy, companionship, excitement, pleasure. Was I a con artist? Did I use the language of love and romance to have my way with her? Was I being polite and loving purely as a means of persuading her to let me have sex? I was a human animal, making love, creating meaning.

At the same time, I was absolutely certain that this was not a one night stand. There was already a feeling of bonding, belonging, identity and commitment that held sway over my desires. It was a willingness by both of us to leap into the abyss. Leaping into love is like leaping into death. You can read all about it, you can imagine it, but then it happens. In surrendering to Aileen that night I was discovering a new part of me, a new way of being in the world.

And yet, if I stand back, I can see, again, that we were two young pawns in a wider, longer struggle between traditional and modern Ireland, between the Catholic Church and its teaching of modesty, chastity and self-denial, and a new age of liberalism, pleasure and self-indulgence.

Making love in Bally Olaf was fine as long as the house was empty. But that did not happen too often. In the summer she found her own solution. It was in the wood beside her house. It was an exotic space, full of paths through yew trees, cedars, pines, rhododendrons and fuchsias. But it had become completely overgrown.

Although a good part of the wood belonged to the family, it was not a private space, particularly for making love. There were huge clumps of bamboos, some of which had grown to 20 metres wide. It was in one of these clumps that she created a love nest. She made the entrance at a point where the bamboos met brambles. To add to the camouflage, she left the outer ring of the first three or four bamboos intact. From there she hacked out a path into the centre. I had no idea she was doing all this. One day as we were walking in the wood, she took out a bandana and tied it round my eyes. She took me by the hand and led me through this obstacle course. It seemed to go on forever. Then she stopped and told me I could take the bandana off. It was weird and wonderful. I was in a bedroom in the middle of the wood. She had cleared a space, cutting the bamboos right down to ground level. She had stripped the leaves from the cut shoots and used them to cover the stalks. On top of the leaves, she had a big piece of plastic. On top of the plastic she had opened out two sleeping bags to form a mattress. She had pillows, sheets and blankets and, to be practical, big plastic bags in which everything could be stored for the next visit.

While the bamboo cocoon was very romantic, it was really only suitable in fine summer weather. Even then it was not as comfortable as a real bed, but bed opportunities were not very frequent. Sometimes we would skip upstairs to her room when we were alone. Her Dad also did us a huge favour by insisting, when the children became teenagers, that they should all have locks on their bedroom doors. The more we got used to making love in her bed, the more we engaged in risky activity. On leaving Kehoe's for the last bus, she would encourage me to go back to Bally Olaf: her parents would still be out and her brothers and sisters would have gone to bed. The temptation was too much. We would inch our way up the stairs, fearful of someone coming out to go to the toilet. It was only a short distance from the top of the stairs to her bedroom door. If I was caught in this space, I would be exposed.

I could only be coming or going to her bedroom. There was a toilet downstairs so what was I doing upstairs?

The only problem with making love after a few drinks was that I was very liable to fall asleep. This is what often happened. One night, I was fast asleep and awoke to find Aileen's hand over my mouth. 'Shush. Mum and Dad have just come in. Quick, under the bed.' I lay there under her bed, naked, clutching my clothes. A couple of minutes later, as Anne checked to see if all her young chicks had come home to roost, there was a knock on the door and a try of the handle 'Are you all right dear?' Aileen waited, pretending to be waking up and in a sleepy voice she called out, 'I'm fine Mum.' And then the relief as Anne walked away. I had to listen for the sound of their bedroom door closing and, after a few minutes, climb back up into her bed. I had to wait a half hour or so to make sure they were asleep before undertaking the precarious trip back through no-man's land, down the stairs and out into the front porch.

I was eventually caught. It was another Saturday night, and once again I woke beside her and realised that it was early morning and time to get up and go. I got my trousers, shirt and jumper on, and decided to avoid noise by putting my shoes on in the small porch outside the front door. I had pulled the door closed behind me and was just putting on my shoes when I saw the lights of the milk delivery van coming down the driveway. There was no escape. If I ran the milkman was sure to see me in his lights. He would probably think I was a burglar and so ring the doorbell and waken the whole house. I decided to play it cool.

I would have liked to have gotten a fag lit and to be smoking nonchalantly as he came into the porch, but there was no time. So I sat down with my back against the door as if I had been put out of the house for being bold, and waited for the milkman to come round the corner into the porch. I looked up and, as if everything was normal, said 'good morning'. In a rush of panic, I realised that he could easily mention this to Anne the next time he called to collect his bill. So I stood up and pleaded with him not to say a word to her. He smiled, nodded, and, as far as I know, never did.

Making love with Aileen was a game of Irish roulette. Condoms were illegal. Trying to get one was like trying to score dope. It was 1970. I was at university. I heard that there was a guy in architecture who sold condoms. I was told to wait for him at 1.00 p.m. at the bend in one of the staircases in Earlsfort Terrace. The price was ten shillings. This was the equivalent of sixteen euro, or four pints of stout. It was expensive, but the luxury of not having to withdraw before I came was something that was well worth the money. I cringe at the thought of the amount of times that I failed to withdraw in time and we went through agony as we waited for her time of month to come round. She suffered from really bad period pain, and yet there were many months, despite her pain, we felt like celebrating.

It was in those moments, those endless moments, of wanting to come, of wanting to please but, at the same time, being conscious of the need for discipline and care, that we made the transition from having sex to making love. I cannot remember once saying to myself, 'ah, fuck it' and exploding inside her. However, there were many times when, before I could do anything, I would have come. There was no elation, rather an immediate sense of remorse. Then the fear set in, and whatever pleasure there had been up until then was wiped out. We would comfort each other, but at the same time there was a rapid attempt to recall the date of her last period, and a calculation of the risk of pregnancy. As the times and years went by, we became more skilled at enjoying the days surrounding her period, and being restrained in the ten days around her cycle. But despite the caution, there would always be the anxious wait for her period to come. It was like living in limbo. Our lives revolved around a monthly statement from her womb.

I would like to think that I am a good lover, but the reality is the legacies of my upbringing are so deeply ingrained in my body and soul that when it comes to physical expression, I am probably closer to a Catholic bishop than to James Bond. I was an eager student, but no amount of learning could overcome my awkwardness in showing affection, in being intimate without being sexual. It is about feeling physically calm and relaxed, about behaving like a lazy ape rather than a frightened boy. Later in life, Aileen would often sidle up to me when I might be in the middle of cooking and she would nuzzle into my arms and demand that I stop what I was doing and hug her. I was awkward and reluctant. This was a game which I was not very good at playing. She would tease me about my immediate wanting to back away. Once she had got me into her arms, and she was nestling in under my shoulder, she would look up and say, 'don't you see how I was made to fit into this space?' And yet, while I longed to give in, something deep inside me prevented me from letting go. I got addled and confused. Was this a form of foreplay? Did she want to make love now in the middle of the kitchen, in the middle of the day, while I was supposed to be cooking? Often she was hurt by my repulsion. But she knew and understood my difficulties. She would refuse to give in. She would come back in and clinch me like a good boxer who had been badly hit but refused to fall.

But there were other times when I did behave like an ape. One of the things I learned from Dad was the appreciation of being scratched. There is something wonderfully erotic about feeling well-trimmed nails making their way across my head, down my neck and along my back. There is an art to being a good scratcher. It is akin to being a good masseur. If the nails are short, and if the movement is not hard enough, it can be frustratingly insipid. If the nails are too long, they do not have enough strength. As with a good massage, there is a fine line between pain and pleasure. It is crucial never to draw blood.

Often, particularly if we were watching television, I would squat down and get Aileen to scratch my head. At other times, in bed, she would scratch my back. Sometimes this went beyond the bounds of delicacy. During the scratching she would be on the feel for a pimple. When she found one, she would go wild with excitement and get me to lie over on my tummy. She would sit straddled across me and while I lay silent and still, she would begin a slow deliberate process of squeezing, digging her nails deeper and deeper into my skin. Then there would be a joyous announcement. 'Oh my god Tom you should see the size of it. It's enormous. It's still coming.' After a few minutes of squeezing and ejaculations of delight, she would get me to lie over and take a look at the so-called crop of puss, and I would see this tiny little squiggle of yellow and green at the end of her nail.

During the time she became ill, and I became fearful that she was going to die, I began to scratch my own head. It was a form of despair. It began to get out of control. If I was sitting at the computer and I stopped writing, my hand would automatically go up to my head. It got so bad that I began to draw blood. It was only when I went to the barber and he stood back in amazement at the sight of my scalp that I managed to stop.

9

I cannot get through to her. I wish there was a way of reaching out to her. I would love to be able to hear her voice, to be in her presence. If only there was some sign that she was happy, resting in peace. I hate the silence of my own thoughts. I seem to disappear into myself. What is the point of memories if you cannot share them? How do I know who I am unless I speak or write? My thoughts and memories have no sustenance, no real value, unless they are expressed or communicated. I may as well be Pepe, my dog, whimpering in the middle of one of her dreams. What do dogs dream of? I have no idea, but I doubt they are consumed by thoughts of life after death. Many times during her last year when the pain became intense, she would get up in the middle of the night to go to the bathroom. As she went past the end of the bed, I would often ask her how she was doing. She would say 'I am fine sweetie.' That is all that I want to hear now.

Trying to speak to the dead, looking for signs of life after death are part and parcel of looking for signs of

God and salvation. I know that I will never see or hear from Aileen again, she is gone forever, but I keep on looking and hoping. Sometimes when I come to the depth of my loneliness, I try to reach out to her, to see if she is somehow back in the bedroom with me, and if I can feel the sense of her being. I try to get beyond my body, to become a spirit. She told me often that she did not believe there was a heaven or hell, but she did believe in spirits, that when you die your spirit continues to linger in the space, sometimes for days, sometimes for years. She said that if it had been a happy, peaceful death, the spirit would feel good and leave the material world. But if it had been a troubled or dishonourable death, then the spirit might linger longer and become a troubled ghost scaring those left behind. I don't think Aileen has caused me any trouble since she died. Neither has Luke, and yet they both died at home. It is perhaps the opposite: I have always felt happy, calm and relaxed when I am at home. It is just that I miss her so much. Maybe there are happy ghosts. I never asked her about that.

Aileen did many things to stay alive. Besides following the anti-cancer regimes of Jane Plant and Nicholas Gonzalez, she went for different treatments: reflexology, reiki, shiatsu and metamorphosis. She told me that the metamorphosis treatments she got from our friend, Miriam, were the best. I have no idea of the principle, but it seems to me to revolve around calming the soul to soothe the body. It is a lovely form of spiritualism, far better than kneeling down, or punishing yourself through suffering pain.

Aileen's most interesting spiritual journeys were her visits to a shaman. He was a quiet, unassuming man who lived in a very small house in a working-class area in a town in Kildare. He certainly was not into spiritual healing for the money. He was the seventh son of a seventh son, and had gone to America to learn how to become a shaman. He was recommended to Aileen by a woman to whom she went for reflexology. She told Aileen that he only took on clients with whom he could work, and that he was very reluctant to take on new ones. When she went to him first, he brought her into his little living room and explained to her that the only way he could know if he could work with her was by sniffing her. So, as she stood still, he began to slowly sniff her up and down, front and back. I think he was ascertaining if she had any bad spirits. She passed the test, and he told her that he did not feel any strong smell of cancer. But there was another test. He would have to come to our house, to see if there were any bad spirits that might be linked to her illness. This was when I met him.

I do not remember much about him, he could have come to fix the plumbing. What I do remember was his complete sense of assuredness. He radiated calmness. And he had the most penetrating green eyes. They were like the eyes of a fox, clear and strong. In those seconds that we were introduced, I thought he was staring into my soul. Aileen had told me that he would have to go round the house and up to our bedroom. If he found anything troubling, he would have to do an exorcism. He had brought all the things that were needed to perform this ritual. Aileen told me I was welcome to stay, but I opted to take Pepe for a walk.

Pepe got a long walk, and when I came back home, he was gone. He had indeed found a bad spirit in the bedroom, over on Aileen's side, but he had performed an exorcism and he assured Aileen that all was fine. He was very optimistic that all of this boded well for her recovery. After she died, I wondered if I should go to see him to see if he could help me make contact with her. Did I need reassurance? Was he a medium I could trust?

A friend, whose wife died not long before Aileen, told me about a woman in Wicklow who was a brilliant medium, as good as any postman or telephone operator. He said that she was a clairvoyant as well as a medium and she would be able to tell me intimate things about myself and Aileen that nobody else could ever have known. She would be able to reach out to her and to tell me how she was.

It was a very attractive proposition. But what if I didn't believe? Sometimes I think that if I close my eyes at night in bed and listen long and hard enough, I can hear Aileen. Would it be the same with the medium? What is it that stops me from trying it out? Am I afraid that if I went once, I could be on the slippery slope into magical thinking? And even if this did happen, and I believed I was able to communicate with Aileen, if it brought me comfort and consolation, why not?

The question then is, if I believed I had made contact, what would we talk about? Would we have to talk, or would it be some form of communication that is beyond language, a form of spiritual being together in which neither of us would have to say anything, it would be just felt? Even stranger, I have often wondered what it would be like if she walked in the door one day as if she was coming in from work?

'Hello, my love,' she would say as always. 'Anything strange or startling?'

'But I thought you had died?'

'Oh, yes, but I thought I would just pop in to reassure you I was all right. There is no need to tell me about anything because I know everything. I just thought you needed to see me.'

'But what was it like to die?'

I wonder what it would be like if I knew in advance that she was going to call in on Sunday night at eight o'clock. I can imagine the build-up, the enormous anticipation of being in her presence, being able to hear her voice. What would we talk about? How long would we have? Would it be like those dreadful phone conversations we used to have in the early days when she or I were in England?

There were many times, particularly at the beginning, when we had to be apart. I hated them, but there was no choice. We were no different from a long line of Irish people who had to leave home to make a living. We were forced back into other forms of communication, of reaching out using the media of phone operators and postmen. We had to express our love through long love-letters and sporadic, rushed phone calls. The letters were full of rambling emotional outpourings. It was as if the pen was a kind of wand that captured my thoughts and emotions but, like all wands, could not be relied on. Sometimes I think that rather than Aileen coming back home, it would be nicer to receive a letter from her.

In the summer of 1970, having been together as a courting couple for nine months, I had to head back over to England to earn money to pay my university fees. Aileen was finishing school and had to sit her Leaving Certificate exams. Soon after I left she wrote:

> *What is it what makes a man and a woman know that they, of all other men and women in the world, belong to each other? Is it no more than chance meeting no more than being alive in the world together at the same time? Is it only a curve of the throat, a line of the chin, the way the eyes are set, a way of speaking, a way of thinking? Or is it something deeper and stranger, something beyond meeting, something beyond chance and fortune? Are there others, in other times of the world, whom we would have loved, who would have loved us? Is there perhaps one soul among all others – among all who have lived, the endless generations from world's end to world's end, who must love us or die? And whom must we love, in turn, whom we must seek all our lives long to search out and find? Finding you, belonging to you there is a reason for what was not. I open my heart to you and because you are not here beside me, breathing the air I breathe, I open my heart also to sorrow. I cannot see or understand you. I am afraid you will not understand me. I shall not be able to write to you for long my love if ever we part for a long time, thoughts are too deep, feelings too passionate to passively lay on paper ...*

And yet we did not have to be apart to write to each other. It was as if letter writing was a different medium for communicating: thoughts and feelings were transcribed differently from when they were spoken. In the winter of '69, having been together for a few months, I wrote to her, even though we were seeing each other every day.

> *You just sit there, and I look at you and smile and I think to myself I'm so lucky, so damn lucky. And then you bow down your head and your face is lost in masses of beautiful hair, and I hold you and I know that I want and need you so much that even those brief seconds so precious seem lost for a while. And then you toss your head back and wipe away the bits of hair that block your eyes and automatically you smile and look at me and I am just looking back at you, and we stare deeply into each other, and then I kiss you, or your hand or arm and try to squeeze all my love into it and you smile mother-like and rub my head, while I dream, enjoy happiness, smile and let love take over my empty mind and curse the time, loving you deeply. And we stay like that, motionless, saying nothing, thinking, dreaming ... I need you; your kindness, warmth, loving smile, your understanding, your sympathy, and, most of all, your love. I want you, both mentally and physically. I am thinking I shouldn't say that. Sex is a word with much good and so much bad meaning attached to it. Bad because of dirty jokes, abuse, misunderstandings, the permissive life where it has become an animal life thing*

done for pure enjoyment and not out of love. Good because of all its meaning, sincerity, pureness, wonderousness, and tenderness. The love it signifies, and manifests.

I like the vulnerability and openness that comes with handwritten letters: emotions seem to shake the words out differently onto the page. It makes reading between the lines easier. You can see the tiredness and frailty of the hand. There is less room to hide, to edit and delete. Aileen's letters were always something more than the words. They had a presence beyond the pages. They were tactile. I could hold them as if I was holding on to her. When she sprayed her perfume onto the pages, I could smell her. There was the pleasure of opening up a letter, feeling the pages between my fingers, knowing that for the next ten or fifteen minutes I was going to go on an emotional journey that would end in tears. I was in her presence again. I could feel her through her words. It was not always important that they made sense. Often the sentences were more like paintings, a kaleidoscope of words whose beauty had to felt and experienced as much as read and deciphered.

Sending and receiving letters was an exercise in delayed gratification. The time delay meant that our letters often crossed in the post. Sometimes I would be reading a letter, and it would take me ages to realise what she was writing about. Other times, without reference, she would wander into thoughts about love, or about family and friends, and it was only after a while that I would realise that she was responding to something I had written.

I came to hate the postman and my dependence on him. He must have known by the steady flow of letters that they were from a loved one. She always wrote 'SWALK' (sealed with a loving kiss) on the back of the envelope. He must have known the hurt that I felt when he passed by my house without a letter, especially when it came to the third or fourth day. And yet he seemed to be oblivious to my feelings. I wanted to scream and shout at him. Even when I met him on the road, he never made any mention of the letters. It was as if he had to play the game of being an impartial postman, an intermediary who treated everything that came into his bag with a sense of confidentiality.

Our phone calls were full of anxiety and frustration. This time the medium was the operator. Yet no matter how short, they were sensational, the softness of her voice, her words of love, her sense of hope and forlornness. It was like jumping into a warm sea of intense feeling and emotion in which we thrashed about for three minutes or so. It did not matter what she said. It was the feeling of being with her in a way that letters could never achieve. I could sense her being, the tremors in her voice, the sighs, the laughs, the smiles. I could feel her tears.

Trying to make a phone call from the middle of England to Ireland from a public phone box was hell. It was the summer of 1970, and I was back sterilising daffodil bulbs and shacking up with the sixty-odd Irish student workers who were working in the nearby pea-canning factory. We lived as migrant workers, housed in tin-roofed huts, sleeping on iron beds with straw mattresses, young men, away from home, missing their families and loved ones. There was one phone on the main road. When it worked, it attracted the young men as if it was the Tardis from *Doctor Who*, or some strange sex machine that had dropped from the heavens. The queues in the evenings and on Sunday were long and relentlessly slow. There was no banter to pass the time. Everyone was too frustrated and exhausted by the process.

I would write to her in advance saying that I would call at a certain time. But that would be days in advance and anything could go wrong in between time. I might have said nine and be still in the queue at half past, knowing that Aileen would be at home, waiting in the study. The hope, the anticipation, and when I did get through, it was all over so quickly.

Getting into the box was only the beginning. There were still enormous hoops to get through. Sometimes the phone in her home would be busy. The operator would come on: 'Sorry caller, I'm getting an engaged tone. Please press button B and try again later.' I would try and explain about the queue and plead with her to try again.

Sometimes it was not just her home phone, but the lines that were busy. At least then the operator would try again without being asked and I could open up the door and apologise for the delay to the next lad in line: it was not my fault. I had to be alert. The second there was an answer from the far end, I had to make a quick decision. The phone call was to Bally Olaf, not to Aileen. If she answered and I could hear her voice, it was all systems go. If one of her parents or sisters answered, I had to decide whether I was going to invest the money and press button A. If I did and she was not there, it was a lot of money down the drain. The cost of a three minute call from England to Dublin was one and a half times my hourly rate of pay.

There was also the problem of putting in the coins. I could never make out how the operator knew how much money I had put in. How was she able to distinguish between the sounds of pennies and shillings? Had she developed a trained ear?

'Insert 5 shillings, caller,' she would say.

But sometimes the coins would not go in or they would be rejected. I would fumble desperately for more coins. All this time I could hear Aileen waiting at the other end. But if I tried to talk to her before the money went in, I could be cut off. Even when the money was in, and the operator was happy, there was still the problem of pressing button A. It could get stuck. I had to be careful to control my feelings. If I banged the button, the operator would cut me off and tell me to press button B. If I did that and started the procedure all over again, the mob outside would be in on top of me.

'I'm sorry operator. I am having a little difficulty in pressing button A.'

There might be a sigh of exasperation but sometimes I would be put through. What then made the emotional swim of love more beautiful was the knowledge that I would be able to press button B at the end, get my money back and enjoy a few free pints.

The feeling of getting through, pressing button A and realising that she was not at home, was heartbreaking. When, later, she was in London, she wrote to me about what happened to her one Sunday night when, having tried to get through for more than half an hour, she phoned my house. I had given up on her and gone to the pub.

> *I stay and am miserable, the longing for you, for everything that is you, surges in on me and crushes me to helplessness, as on Sunday when I rang and you were not there, your father was talking to me, I was so upset I started roaring crying and I couldn't answer a word you father said. I tried and my voice came out so high. He asked if there was something wrong, but I don't want to think about it.*

Most operators were dull and boring, formal and official. It was as if they had been trained to be miserable, unsympathetic, hard-hearted creatures. They played it by the book, probably afraid that some higher authority, an overseer, was looking over them behind their back. She and I would be chatting away and the dreaded voice would come in. 'I am sorry, caller. I am going to have to ask you to finish now.' I wanted to scream and shout, but instead let Aileen plead for a little more time. When she was on song and the operator's heart had not been turned to stone through organisational mangling, we might be given one or two more minutes. A few times, we encountered operators with hearts of gold who would let us stay on for ten, fifteen, twenty minutes. One night we were together for over an hour. So we lived in hope.

Tonight the operator will let us speak a little longer because he knows perhaps what love is or if he doesn't he is very jealous and wants to find out. I will then thank him. I will hope for him secretly that he knows and feels love as much as I do for you.

The end of each letter, the end of each phone call, was a small death. I was alone again, feeling lost. I was able to imagine where she was, what she was doing, whom she was with. She presided in her absence. There was the certainty that I would see her again. I could live with that.

10

We were still young in the summer of 1970, I was nineteen, she was seventeen. While we were both very attached to our family and friends, we wanted to get out of Ireland. We saw ourselves as young cosmopolitans, anxious to see the world, or at least Europe. We planned a major trip to Greece. The Greek islands had attained mythical status. There was the promise of blue skies, swimming in the warm sea, sunbathing on the beach, drinking ouzo and retzina, and falling asleep under the stars. It was exotic and erotic. It was a place to explore our sexuality. We could not afford the plane or airfare, so we decided we would have to hitchhike. We did not want to stay in hostels – that would have meant sleeping separately – so we bought a tent. Aileen got permission from her parents. It was a big leap forward for them. They were strongly against the idea, but there was no embargo: they weren't that shocked or angry. For us it was a pilgrimage, a journey across Europe to the land of sunshine, hedonism and eternal youth.

We made good progress through Germany and Austria, over to Trieste and, from there, to the

Yugoslav border. There was a long queue for those who did not have visas. Ireland was a good Catholic country and did not recognise communist Yugoslavia. But we were fortunate: a young man appeared from nowhere. He was a local but spoke good English. He explained what we had to do to buy a visa. He helped us change our money. It was even better when he said he was going our way and that he could give us a lift to Rijeka. After a couple of hours on the road, we stopped off in a tavern where he insisted on buying us food, beers and some local plum brandy. Nevertheless, I was being careful with him: I thought that he might try and get me drunk, perhaps even spike my drink, and try to make off with Aileen. But I was wrong: he got us drunk, but made off with our passports and traveller's cheques. In a moment, everything changed. Greece was hundreds of miles away, and we were stuck in a tavern somewhere in Yugoslavia with little money and no identification.

We eventually got a lift to Rijeka. It was late. We were tired and frightened. We went to the police station. We felt sure that, once we explained what had happened, they would be full of sympathy, would give us some food and allow us to sleep in a cell. But we may as well have been vagrants arriving into a five star hotel. It was quite a shock coming from the cocoon of Western society to this land of pitiless communists who seemed to have no idea of Christian charity. They stared blankly at us as if we were some curious form of human animal that had wandered in off the street. Nobody spoke English. When I made a feeble gesture of wanting to sleep by putting my hands to the side of my head, they laughed loudly. When they got tired of our gestures, they ordered us out of the station.

We went to the bus station. It was closed. We went back down town. While Aileen waited outside, I went into different cafes, going up and down the bar, asking if anyone spoke English. Rijeka is a big, industrial port. Eventually in one bar a man responded: 'Liverpool.' I was elated. But all he kept saying was 'Liverpool.' He was obviously a sailor, and obviously very drunk.

He wanted to buy me a drink. I communicated that I no money, no passport, that they had been stolen. I pointed to the door and went back out to Aileen and we waited. Shortly afterwards he came out. He gesticulated to follow him. We followed. A woman came running up the street behind us and she grabbed Aileen. Pointing to our new found friend, she kept shouting 'No, no, no.' He came back and, while they shouted at each other, Aileen and I had a quite conference. What were we to do? I told her we had no option but to go back with him. I would not leave her alone.

His flat consisted of a small kitchen, a living room, a bathroom and one bedroom. It all seemed very ordinary. He brought us into the kitchen and we sat down at the table, and while we ate some bread and cheese, he tried to ply us with drink. It was an intense fifteen minutes. The communication was basic. We did not understand anything each other said. We relied on gestures. We kept putting our two hands together and laying our heads against them. He eventually relented and showed us to his bedroom. This was an extraordinary piece of work. It was as if he had learnt a thing or two from all the brothels in all the ports in the world he had visited. He was obviously very passionate about what he did. This was no lazy sailor. The *pièce de résistance* was the bed, which was neatly made with brown satin sheets. The windows had deep, green velvet curtains. The walls were painted in dark red. On each side of the bed there was a table with matching lamps that with the flick of the switch went from white, to green, to red. On the ceiling over the bed there was a big mirror. He was delighted. 'You like?' he asked. He smiled with excitement. We might have thought that we were sophisticated cosmopolitans off to see the world, but in reality we were very naïve and innocent, with no experience of sex for the sake of sex.

Aileen and I stood in awesome silence. Sensing our lack of enthusiasm, he went to the drawer of one of the bedside tables and took out a bunch of porn magazines. He sat on the bed and opened them up. I was amazed by the graphic images. I had never had the courage to search out anything beyond what could be seen in the magazines on the top shelf in the shops in London. I might have travelled through Spain, France and England, but I was still an innocent Catholic boy who suffered from guilt and shame.

We immediately made for the door. He protested. It was time for a grand Catholic gesture. I told Aileen that we should immediately drop to our knees beside the bed and start praying. I told her not to lift up her eyes. After a few Hail Marys, our prayers were answered and our sailor friend left. We waited for ages before getting into bed.

As soon as we woke in the morning, we got up and dressed. We went into the kitchen and made some coffee and waited for him to waken. He was still the same gruff sailor, hung over, but obviously remorseful. I mentioned the police and he agreed to take us to the station. There he explained what had happened. This time they made a phone call to someone who spoke English. She told us that we would have to get to Zagreb where there was an English consulate. We had no choice but to hitch.

For two weeks we lived in a tiny bedroom with a shared bathroom and a small daily food allowance while the Irish government verified that we were who we said we were. Word eventually came through, and we were given the tickets and money to get back to London. It was during those two weeks that Aileen and I discovered that we could live together. We talked and walked during the day. It was a journey of mutual discovery. It was as if the Greek gods had intervened and sent us to a place of penitential practice.

Aileen was as much naïve as she was sexually adventurous. In the spring of 1971, she went to live in London. It was another stage in the game of attraction. Like millions of Irish before her, she was a young woman looking for work and accommodation. She was an innocent abroad. She was looking for a job in a hotel because she felt that they might have accommodation included. Someone had mentioned the name of a hotel. When she got there, she discovered it would not be opening for another few weeks. She got into conversation with the owner.

It was funny because when I told him I was Irish we got into a real long conversation on contraceptives ... when I was going he asked me was I okay for money so I said I was for the moment so he said if I was short to say so to him. I still don't understand that cos I mean he doesn't really kind of know me and he has been so openly generous. I mean I did start getting ideas about how in his mind I might earn it but I certainly doubt that, he was to me okay, I mean okay fine.

She eventually did get work as a chambermaid in the St George Hotel and ended up sharing an attic room with three other girls.

Maybe it's lucky I'm a fairly light sleeper. Last night it was just after three I woken when I heard our door open and the light was turned on quickly, it clicked when I realised it was none of us as we were all in. This man had come in and shut the door behind him. He was the receptionist who works in the hotel. He's about 26 – or so. He fancies himself so much he's sick. I just watched him come in and close the door and he went over to the other Irish girl's bed. At this stage I just kind of sat up and looked 'cos I couldn't believe it. He sat down at the side of her bed and just started at her with his hands under the blanket. I just dashed and turned the light on, his eyes unbelievably innocent and frightened, like a little boy caught doing something wrong. Everyone woke up immediately and just couldn't believe it. Your man just ended up backing out of the room saying 'I can see I'm not wanted here.'

That summer, I went to work in Wisbech in Cambridgeshire, about ninety miles north of London. It was one of the many small canning factories that operated around East Anglia during the season. The factory specialised in canning strawberries, and was different because it was managed and run by Irish students. It was a hotbed of fresh young bodies, yearning for romance and sex. At night, after the pub closed, young drunks climbed up to the loft, to sit and lie on mattresses, drink warm beer, to fondle and be fondled, to lay and be laid.

Aileen had heard all about it. She wanted to come up for the season but she did not want to give up her full-time job in London. One Saturday morning, I got a message from the factory office to say that she was on her way up. She had gotten up early and taken a bus out to the A10 from where she hitched. It was a hot summer day. She took a shoulder bag, wore sandals, a short skirt and a sleeveless t-shirt with '69' emblazoned on the front. She made it up to Wisbech in three hours. She swore to me that she thought '69' referred to the year. On Sunday evening, I brought her out to the road to hitch back to London. She wrote to me when she got back.

Tom why is today over already? When you kissed me goodbye and turned away, I walked on for a while because I didn't want to go. And cars go so quickly, to take me so quickly from you, so I walked; then how I hated having to get into that first car ... And I think of us then walking on a road today and a horrid sensation shook me which I have never known before, I don't suppose you were very far out on the road but I thought you were and a car sped past ... My love, my love, my love I wish you were here to hold me, I so desperately need you to hold me, all of what is me which is little is yours and all what I feel which is great is for you forever.

Hold my hand and we're lost in a forest.
There are no paths, there is no time.
Eternity stretches before us.

11

Try as I may, I cannot get back to how I felt then. I want to go back and relive the experience, to be in my body and mind at that time, in that space. I want to do what I did, say the same things, experience the same emotions. I was innocent. I did not realise that those intense feelings of love, mixed up and confused as they may have been, are what I chased for the rest of my life. It is to have that overwhelming sensation of being engulfed, of being swept off my feet, being somewhere between lost and found. I try to become as still and remote from the present as possible, to let my mind transpose itself back to those moments, to be in her presence, to be able to hold her. And yet I know that all that has happened in between, all the experiences that I have had, have destroyed the possibility of ever recapturing that time. I am disillusioned? Was that time pure being? Can I not move on and have new fulfilling experiences? Am I to spend the rest of my life trying to recapture that which is lost forever? I seem to have spent much of my early years with Aileen creating loving feelings and emotions, and most of my later years trying to keep them alive.

We longed to have our own space and privacy in which we could have peaceful sex, make love and play at being romantic. The problem was that we were students without funding or part-time work. It was not until I qualified with my degree and got a job – as an interviewer on a survey research study – that there was a possibility of doing things differently. As soon as I got my first pay packet, Aileen went on the hunt for a bedsit. The one she found was in Grosvenor Square in Rathmines, a small, terraced house converted into a warren of bedsits. It was our first real love nest, a place where we could be without the supervisory eye of our parents, sisters and brothers. It was a tiny room, a single bed, a sink, a table, and little else.

The second weekend into our nesting, it was nearly four o'clock in the morning and there were six other people sitting around the floor, with drained bottles of beer and stout, ashtrays full of the ends of cigarettes and joints. Very few of our friends were working, most were students, most were living at home, and most were dependent on bedsits, flats, 'free houses' or a party, to go to after the pubs closed. So, when we were standing outside Kehoe's that Saturday night, it was impossible to refuse the pleas of these pub refugees. We had invited them to come back and inspect our new nest. They were full of promises that they would be out by 1.00 a.m.

That weekend was pivotal in terms of my career. I was in the running for a job as a research assistant for a major Irish trade union. I had been in for an interview, then for psychological testing, then for another interview. The interview panel were divided between myself and another candidate, so they called us both in on the Friday afternoon and asked us to write an essay on the current tripartite talks (unions, employers and government) for the future of the Irish trade union movement. I woke up early on Sunday, cycled home and worked frenziedly all night to get the essay finished. I got it finished, but I didn't get the job.

But I had my interviewing job, and I was flush with money, so we decided to make the leap forward and get married. We told our parents. They were gracious. They too were nice and said they were delighted. Aileen was a first year student in art college. My job was temporary, at best for six months. All we had – and everyone seemed reasonably convinced about this – was our love for each other. So we ran our campaign of persuasion on love being more important than prospects. We won their hearts, but there was consternation when we said we wanted to get married sooner rather than later. There was shock when we said the beginning of March, six weeks later.

'Is everything all right?' they asked. We kept repeating that we were fine. This did not work, so we had to state emphatically that Aileen was not pregnant. 'So why the rush?' We kept repeating the mantra that we were in love and wanted to be together. We did not have the courage to say that we were sick of operating in clandestine times and spaces, of not being able to have free, unrestrained sex whenever we wanted.

So the search for a new love nest began. Again, Aileen did the searching. She came up with something on Whitton Road in Terenure. It was the top half of a small, redbrick terrace house. The house was divided into two. There was a young couple with a baby in the downstairs rooms. We had the upstairs rooms. At the top of the stairs, there was a little room on the return. In most houses on the road, this tiny box room operated as a bedroom. For us, it was our kitchen. There was an ancient gas stove, a sink with one cold tap in the middle, a metal press and a small table at which two people could just about sit. The window overlooked a small, overgrown garden. There was a single light socket. There was no fridge.

On the same first landing, there was a tiny bathroom which consisted of a bath and a toilet. There was no washbasin. The bathroom was shared with the young family below. On up four more steps and to the left was our bedroom, which was dominated by the huge double bed that we inherited from Aileen's parents. Straight ahead was our living room. We also inherited a table and four chairs. There was no phone, no television, no sound system. I had grown up accustomed to living without. We did not get a fridge in Ardtona until the beginning of the 1960s. I had learnt from Mum how to shop each day for fresh meat, fish and vegetables, how to keep milk and butter cool in a bucket of cold water in summer. The reality was that Aileen and I were well off. Many young married couples in those days had to live with their parents. Aileen and I had three rooms. The rent was £5 a week. We had £20 a week to live on.

If our parents were not very happy about our rush into marriage, neither were our friends. When we announced our forthcoming marriage in Kehoe's, there was no rush to hugs and kisses and cries of congratulations, no 'oohing' and 'aahing' at her engagement ring. There was a reserved silence. No matter how we dressed it up, we were seen as capitulating to the system. We were on the slippery slope to a semi-detached house in the suburbs, two kids, and a mortgage. If things went on like this, I was told that I would soon be coming into Kehoe's in a suit, shirt and tie with Aileen pushing a pram behind me. There was a fear that we would become moralistic and give out about drugs and drinking. If it continued we could end up joining Fianna Fáil. There was an air of suspicion and distrust, but nothing direct was said. We were teased and ridiculed. It was the usual Irish mixture: serious things were said in a joking manner.

Some of us, more than others, were willing to play the game of free love. It was an ideal to which we aspired, but it brought so much emotional baggage that few of us lapsed Catholics were really able to live up to it. It is probably more demanding than celibacy. We could say the words – if you cannot be with the one you love, love the one you're with. It was a mantra of the swinging sixties. It was a real test of how much you had shaken off the shackles of Catholic Ireland. It might have been great if free love did not generate such strong feelings of sexual jealousy.

Aileen and I were a symbolic threat. We wanted good love more than free sex. We wanted each other. We wanted the freedom of living together, but we also wanted security and public recognition. We may have been against the system, but we were not going to be martyrs for the cause. We could not survive on the thin air of ideological rhetoric that wafted around south Dublin and mixed so easily with the dope smoke. We needed each other.

We had no option but to go for a church wedding. Even if there was a registry office, it would have been beyond the bounds of acceptability to go there. While there were the beginnings of cultural revolution against the Catholic Church in Ireland in the early 1970s, it would have been too much of a leap for our parents. It would have driven a wedge between them and us. So, if we were going to capitulate to the system, we decided to get it over and done quickly, as if it was some form of execution. There would be no hotel reception, but a small party back in her house. There would be fifty or sixty guests, but only three of our friends. There would be no stag or hen party. Instead, we would meet with some friends in Kehoe's the night before. It was a low-key affair, more like an emigrant's wake than a celebration.

I managed to avoid our marriage banns being announced. This was the process whereby, during the four weeks prior to our wedding, an announcement had to be made in my local parish church asking if anyone knew why we should not be allowed to marry. This would have delayed the wedding. So having an aunt who was a lay nun, and well-connected in the Church, and a grand-uncle who had been one of Archbishop McQuaid's key supplicants, I managed to get an exemption. The compromise, however, was that I had to visit the local curate to sign some forms. He ushered me into the front living room. Having gone through the forms and the formalities, he sat back in his chair, looked at me, and asked, like everyone else, what was all the rush. I repeated the mantra. He was not buying it. He was concerned. In that lovely, priestly manner, with his arms resting on the side of the chair and his hands joined at the fingertips, he asked the big question.

'Do you mind me asking, Tom, have you any experience of women?'

I was flummoxed and thought for a moment he was going to ask me if I was still a virgin.

'How do you mean, father?' I asked.

'Well, do you know how to treat a woman, how to look after her?'

I was relieved, but still confused.

'In what way, father?'

'Well, Tom, let me tell you that women like the odd treat every now and then.'

'Like how, Father?' I asked.

'Like a new bonnet at Easter.'

Aileen and I wanted to be cool. We wanted to distance ourselves from the bourgeois, Catholic culture in which we had been inculcated. We were desperate to send out signals that we were not really that committed to getting married. We met up with Tom Hobson, my best man, in our new flat in Whitton Road on the morning of our wedding. We smoked a couple of joints and drank a couple of gin and tonics. Aileen did not want a white wedding. In the weeks since we announced our forthcoming nuptials, she had been busy. She made her own wedding dress, in her favourite colour: purple. It was a halter neck under which she wore a lighter purple long-sleeved blouse. She also made me my wedding outfit: a three-quarter length deep green velvet jacket with which I wore a white shirt with a green string velvet tie. Tom, my best man, went for the Tiny Tim look. He had a three-quarter length tweed jacket. Both he and I had long hair. His was way past his shoulders. I had a long, wispy moustache.

We did not arrange for any photographs. It was as if we wanted no record; there would only be hearsay accounts and rumours of what had happened that day. However, some friend of her parents, who was big into cameras, made a short colour 16 mm film of the ceremony. It had all the jerks and jaggedness of silent black and white movies. It showed the scene inside the church and outside as the guests mingled together. Aileen was so obviously in command. She is in front of me, eyes bright and determined. She is striding out of the church, holding my hand tightly, taking me to the promised land.

Years later, I was rummaging in the study in Ardtona and came across a black and white photo. I did not recognise the space. It was in some modern living room; there were all these people standing around a couch. It seemed recent. But I did not recognise any of them. There was none of my family there. What intrigued me was that there were four priests in the photograph, all in dog collars. My eye was drawn down to the middle of the photograph, and there were Aileen and I, sitting in the middle of the couch. It was the obligatory photo taken at the wedding party of all Aileen's relatives with the happy couple, blessed by the presence of many priests.

Our honeymoon was another attempt at being alternative. We spent a week together down in a small lock house on the River Barrow in Carlow that my uncle Sean and Auntie Rosemary lent us. It was early March. It was freezing cold, but there was a huge fireplace and hearth. It was a blast from the past. We had no car. Each day we did the three-quarter hour walk along the towpath into Graiguenamanagh to do our shopping and have a couple of drinks before heading back to the lock house, where there were no sounds except the birdsong, the mooing cattle, and the ongoing gurgle from the flow of water through the canal locks.

The first few months of our marriage were far from easy. I was still working as a social survey interviewer. I had to work afternoons and evenings, slogging through the suburbs of Dublin trying to persuade the rump of the chosen sample of people to participate. Often I did not get home until after eleven o'clock. I would have spent the day knocking on doors and asking strangers allow me interview them about their prejudices. It was mentally and physically draining. Aileen was disappointed when I came home worn out. She would have been waiting, anxious to play the part of the romantic, loving wife. She would be full of talk and excitement, but I would be silent and morose. In the morning, she would get up and go to art college before me. She was operating in a different world. We really only met at weekends. It is hard to make love in these conditions. The romantic edge began to wear off. The drudgery of married life was getting to us both. Suddenly we were alone, in at the deep end. It was a crucial test. Instead of being able to bring to the surface our feelings and emotions and talk about what was happening, we buried them. The air began to seep from Aileen's balloon of love. She became deflated. The child in her was suffering a rude awakening. She wanted to play at being married. It was all supposed to be good fun. What had happened?

She became desperate. She could not bear what was happening. She followed me to work one day. I came out to find her waiting on the street. She was crying. I had to go out to Drumcondra to keep an appointment with a survey respondent. She said she would come with me. I pleaded with her to have sense. I was getting embarrassed. I was afraid that people who worked with me would see us. She kept on trying to hug and hold on to me. I walked over to O'Connell Street. I waited at the bus stop. She waited with me. I could not talk. I was frightened. I got on the bus, so did she. I told her that this was crazy. She was in floods of tears. I pleaded with her to get off. She did at the next stop. When I got home later that night she could not talk about what had happened. Years later she told me that she was on the verge of leaving and going home.

We may have learnt to make love and be with each other that time we were marooned in Zagreb, but it is more difficult to play the game when there are demands of work, study, family and friends. We liked to think of ourselves as ideal, consummate lovers but the reality was that we lacked experience in dealing with and expressing our feelings and emotions. The other problem was that we were not able to share our problems with our friends. How could we express feelings with them when we could not express them to each other?

While we might have thought otherwise, we were as emotionally immature as the rest of the nation.

But we made it. I got a new job as a research assistant on a national survey of religious beliefs, values and practices. For many months, I had regular office hours. We fell into more regular routines. It was less what we talked about – there was still a great difficulty in being able to talk about feelings and emotions – and more what we did for each other. There was the pleasure of giving and taking, supporting and encouraging, laughing and joking, cooking, eating and drinking and, most of all, being able to climb into bed together at night, make love, wake up in the morning, and make more love. At the weekends we barely got out of bed. There was a routine on Sunday morning of taking turns to go out and get the papers and the comics (*Beano*, *Dandy*, *Bunty*, *Judy* and *Mandy*) and we would linger in bed until lunchtime.

12

She presides in her absence. I can feel her looking at me, distraught and grief-ridden, her knowing sigh, her disappointment at my despair. I try to talk to Arron and Olwen to express my feelings, but every time I start, I cannot stop the tears. It is safer and more comforting to be on my own, to live in the past. I imagine them stuck in their own grief, in their beds, lying awake like me, all of us going over and over what has happened, all that they have lost. It is overwhelming, beyond words. We walk around the house like zombies, staring blankly into space, smiling congenially, saying nothing, feeling everything.

Arron is lucky. He has found Jenni. Olwen has only me. What is it like for a young teenage girl, sweet sixteen, to lose her mother? I long for Aileen to hold her hand, to guide her through these coming years as she moves through the minefields of love and romance, reassuring her about her beauty, praising her choice of dress, laughing at her choice of earrings, worrying about her shoes, chiding her about her silliness, calming her when she is fearful or troubled. She is the same age as Aileen was when I first met her. She is as beautiful as Aileen.

There is an art to being beautiful and attractive. It is a balance between being seductive and glamorous without becoming an object of lecherous looks. Aileen loved being beautiful, showing herself off, being eye-catching. She was an erotic tease. She played with women as much as men. She learnt these social skills as a young girl.

As a teenager at home, she wanted to be sexy and adventurous, but she had to overcome the disapproval of her parents, particularly her Dad. Paddy took huge pride in the beauty of his four daughters, but was dismayed when any of them wore black, and strict when they tried to wear mini-skirts. This posed problems for Aileen who realised early on that 'little black dresses' were the best for her. She developed a strategy. When we were leaving from her house, she would get ready upstairs in her bedroom, put on her mini and a long cardigan. She would then come downstairs and pull the mini down around her knees. She would get me to go in first into the living room where Paddy and Anne would be watching television. She would stand still for the inspection and then waddle out and, as we walked down the avenue, she would hoist her skirt back up. It was a skill she perfected. Many years later she re-enacted it, waddling past the Swiss Army guard on our way into St Peter's in Rome.

Aileen worked hard at making herself beautiful. She did not have a Hollywood body. It was white, soft and rounded, like a Botticelli statue. She loved Fellini-like images of women, big and full of curves, with large, voluptuous breasts and huge buttocks. But she did not like to see herself that way: she hated if I hesitated in response to her question 'Do you think I am fat?' or 'Do I look fat in this dress?' She had small, neat feet. She had good legs but not long, sleek and elegant. She had curvy hips, a fulsome bottom, a small, round stomach and neat breasts. Most of all, perhaps, her real beauty lay in the quality of her skin. It was soft, almost translucent. The trick, she said, was to never put anything on her face other than warm water.

This was the body with which she had to work. She took pleasure in looking good. She knew that the advantages of a well-fitting suit or dress could be easily enhanced by the right mascara, eye-liner, lipstick, necklace and earrings. They would immediately draw the viewer towards her best features.

Getting ready for work was generally a quick affair, about fifteen minutes. But when it came to a major social occasion – a wedding, party, dinner or night out on the town – the preparation was meticulous. It would start with a long, hot bath. She would come down to the bedroom wrapped in towels. She would begin the process of picking out the potential clothes she might wear that evening. She would have mulled this over in the bath. There may have been three or four contenders which were taken out from the wardrobe and laid out on the bed. Then she would look through her jewellery. She had a penchant for long earrings and complex necklaces that drooped between her neck and breasts. She loved sparkle, in necklaces, broaches and earrings, but not in rings. It was a cultivated pleasure, putting together the different combinations. It was no different from when she played at dressing up as a child, except it was for real. For her, it was always about colour and flamboyance. She could spend an hour lost in this other world. She could become exasperated, even to the stage of asking my advice. If I told her she would look gorgeous in anything, I would get a smouldering, dismissive look. On the other hand, if I really engaged, if I made apposite and useful comments about the advantages of this combination over that, she would glow. I was willing to play her game and she rewarded me with a warm, loving smile.

Once the dress was chosen, there were decisions to be made about potential accompaniments, maybe a cardigan, shawl or scarf. She had a small but exotic collection of antique handbags. Then it was time to make-up her eyes. This was meticulous as, whatever about her clothes and jewels, Aileen drew you to her through her eyes. They were her dazzlers. She wore lipstick, but this was never applied with any great care or precision. Often it was left until we were just going out the door, or in the car.

There were many times when her self-absorption and indulgence drove me mad. We could never agree on a time to leave. I have always been a bit anal retentive about punctuality: I like to arrive on time. An invitation for eight means arriving between ten and twenty past. For Aileen it meant at least half past eight. So I would be ready and waiting downstairs, shuffling around, not able to read or write. I was like a dog listening to its master's footsteps, trying to interpret noises from above. Is she coming yet?

She didn't like to be the first to arrive: there would be no dramatic entry. She loved arriving when everyone was gathered, all the eyes turning to her, the conversations being put on hold, the greetings, the smiles and laughter, the comments from other women on her dress and jewellery. She adored the attention. She loved to dangle herself in front of men, smiling, laughing, cajoling, touching. She loved to engage, to tease, and have fun. She was born to flirt.

Sometimes, when I got too exasperated waiting for her, I had a word with myself, and, persuading myself to calm down, would roll and smoke a small joint. Soon my anger and frustration would give way to lust. I would become cunning. I would stay downstairs until I was reasonably certain that she was almost complete. I would sit at the kitchen table taking pleasure in imagining tasting and feeling her. I would go upstairs into the bedroom and she would realise that something had changed: there was no sign of exasperation, no tone of admonishment. I would walk over to her, looking at her longingly. She never got exasperated. She would simply smile, put on her seductive look, and ask 'have you been smoking?' It was an invitation to heaven. I would say nothing but lean in and kiss her. I would slowly peel away the clothes and jewellery that she had spent hours carefully assembling.

It was a beautiful sacrilege, slowly undoing all that she had spent so long carefully constructing. Making herself beautiful was not that different from making art. It was about working within a given frame and using whatever materials are available to create something that is not just beautiful but imaginative and challenging. And yet, as with art objects that she presented to others, no sooner did she present herself to me than I began the process of deconstruction.

Other times I preferred to come upon her just after she had come down from the bathroom as she glided around the bedroom in her towels, going from the wardrobe, to her jewellery, to the mirror and back again. I liked the way the towels so easily fell to the ground revealing her soft skin, still warm and tingling from the bath.

Those moments of bliss seem to extend out beyond time, beyond death. I try to recapture them as if, in doing so, I could relive the intensity. But no matter how vivid my imagination, no matter how aroused I might be, I can never take pleasure in those memories. There is something sacred about them. It had always been that way, a violation to think of her, to imagine her, to make love to her without her.

Aileen had a strong sexual appetite. She introduced me to pornography, bringing back copies of *Hustler* from London. She was turned on by being able to see other women's vaginas; 'you can see all the pink bits.' She used these magazines regularly to enjoy herself. I naively thought that it was only men who took pleasure in themselves. I was a little taken aback when I came back home unexpectedly one day to find Aileen in bed with the magazines spread open and her homemade dildo lying beside her – a piece of wood that she had honed herself with a condom stretched over it. The reality was that while I used to always say that it was not the wand that makes the magician, and while I liked to think of myself as a great lover, in those early days I was not that skilled in helping Aileen have an orgasm.

She was interested in adventurous sex. Again, it never really occurred to me as something that would be exciting. It was after midnight, and we were in the metro in Paris on our way back to the hotel. She had been working there during the summer of 1974. I had arrived that day, and she had taken me to the erotic film *Histoire d'O*. We had gone back to the hotel room and drank a bottle of champagne, before heading out for something to eat. Aileen was snuggling up to me and then she looked up and saw that the carriage was empty. She waited until the next stop and calmly removed her knickers and sat on top of me. She laughed in between kissing and licking me. We had made love earlier so there was no urgency; we were playing an erotic game. She wanted to make love anywhere and everywhere. Her sexual tap was open full; there was no way I could turn it off. I had to go with the flow.

The great thing about our sex in the early days was that we seemed to be fucking the Church out of our system. The Church had infiltrated our bodies, colonised and subverted our desires and pleasures. Ironically, I was working for the Church at the time as a Research Officer. It was confusing and embarrassing working for an institution which wielded so much power, and yet steadfastly refused not just to change, but to even question its power.

It was early in January in 1976, and I was at a research meeting with some bishops. The main item on the agenda was the formation of a committee of well-known committed lay Catholics who would make suggestions as to how the Irish Church should adapt to the modern world. We had concluded the meeting and were trying to fix a date for the next one. Bishop Jim Kavanagh was sitting beside me and, as he had forgotten his diary, he was looking into mine. Aileen had given me a diary as a Christmas present. I did not know she had tampered with it. At the meeting the search for a date moved out of February into March. As I turned the next page, there was nothing entered for the whole week, except for the Monday where Aileen had written 'Sex with Aileen' – she had chosen a selection of arbitrary dates throughout the year. I didn't say a word but, very quickly, Bishop Kavanagh (who had a good sense of humour) smiled mischievously, and said:

'Sorry, Tom's busy that day.'

He said nothing to me. I have often wondered what he thought. I imagine he might have thought we were planning a family.

It is hard now to understand the stranglehold that the Catholic Church and its loyal missionaries had over the sexual lives of Irish people. Aileen and I may have moved far away from such a discourse and mentality but, having grown up in such a culture, the Church had left its religious footprints all over our bodies and souls. In May 1984, I finished my PhD in the United States and had come home with a small stash of condoms. By August I had run out, and I was trying to buy some on my way to spend a two week holiday down in Brittas Bay in County Wicklow. Everyone knew the monopoly that the Church had over sexual morality. The sale of condoms had been legalised in 1979, but there were strange strings attached. They could only be sold in chemist shops, to *bona fide* married couples who had obtained a doctor's prescription. However, chemists who morally objected to condoms were not obliged to sell them.

I called into the chemist in Dundrum shopping centre, where the assistant looked more embarrassed than I did when I asked for a packet of condoms, brandishing my doctor's prescription. No, they did not stock them. Furious, because the shop was busy and I had been kept waiting, I left and drove on to Enniskerry. Now the tension was building. I was already late. I began to think that if the chemist in Dundrum did not stock them, there was a strong possibility that the one in Enniskerry wouldn't either. What then? Back to *coitus interruptus* for the holiday? Surely not. What a way to have to behave after eleven years of marriage. I was already dejected by the time I arrived at the counter. 'I don't suppose you stock condoms?' 'No, we don't,' came the curt reply. Onwards, but it was getting late, it was Friday afternoon; chemist shops would be closing soon. I wondered if I should make a detour to Bray, a large town which would have a number of chemists. I decided to take a gamble. I knew there were at least two chemists in Wicklow town. My only hope was that one would sell them. It was close to closing time as I walked into the shop, and there, stacked blatantly beside the cash register, were stacks of condoms of different makes and varieties. It was a wonderful, brazen display of secular liberal Ireland.

13

Each generation has its own sense of arrogance, believing that they have escaped from history and have torn off the shackles of the repressive culture in which they were ensnared. When Aileen and I set off for the States in 1979, we were convinced that we were sexually liberated. We saw ourselves as sophisticated Europeans, young urban cosmopolitans who had survived Catholic Ireland and were on a pilgrimage to the mid-West to shine light into the dark recesses of redneck American culture. It turned out to be a bit different.

The call of America was greater for Aileen than it was for me. As with Greece some years earlier, there had been stories in Kehoe's by friends who had been to the States. And there had been the Americans, mostly from an Irish background, who came to visit and invited us back. But Aileen did not want just to visit, she wanted to go and live. She wanted to study in an American university. She insisted there were loads of opportunities to get funding. I was sceptical. We were settling down into the comforts of Dublin middle-class life. We had spent three years renovating our house in Whitton road. Aileen had just finished her degree. She was pregnant with Arron. I had finished my master's degree. I was in a well-paid job. In September 1978, she persuaded me to go on a fact-finding mission.

We were determined to go to New York. We had interviews lined up in the universities. Everyone was amenable about us coming, and we got many tentative offers of places. But there was no funding or facilities. Even if we both got part-time jobs we could not afford the rent of an apartment, let alone the cost of any childcare.

A couple of years previously, Aileen had met John from Southern Illinois University. He took a shine to her. He told her that any time we ever thought of coming to study in the States we would be most welcome to come to SIU. When Aileen had written to say we were coming over, he invited us to come and stay with him, and check out the university and its facilities. So we went to a drive-share agency in New York and linked up with an actress who was moving to Dallas. She brought us as far as Nashville. We had to stay overnight in a motel, which meant that we could not afford the Greyhound bus, so we decided to try and hitch the last two hundred miles. We were out on the road early, trying to make the last two hundred miles up to Carbondale.

I had spent an hour doing my best to get a lift before Aileen took over. She decided to look for sympathy and display her six month womb to the passing drivers. It seemed to work immediately. A middle-aged couple stopped and, as Aileen approached to tell them our destination, the woman starting berating her. When I came up to the car with the two rucksacks, she turned to me and told me that I was a disgrace putting my pregnant wife out on the road hitching. She wound up the window and they drove off.

It was a baptism into the moral contradictions of America. Carbondale may be in Illinois, but it is in the heart of the mid-West, about 100 miles from St Louis. There is nothing much else to Carbondale except the university. In the late seventies, it was a liberal oasis in the middle of American fundamentalism. When the local lads got bored, they would pile into the back of a pick-up and drive into town with a few packs of beer cans and throw empty, half empty or sometimes full cans at the students. As they drove home out of the town, they often took out their guns to shoot at the road signs.

When we eventually arrived, John collected us from a diner and brought us back out to his house. He lived out of town. We stopped off in a supermarket on the way home. We thought John was shopping to cook dinner, but when he came out all he had were two large flagons of Californian wine and huge bags of potato chips. It was Sunday afternoon; it was the middle of the football season. Instead of ambling around the leafy streets of Carbondale, we were stuck out in the middle of nowhere. John seemed to have lost all interest in Aileen. I thought that it must have been that she was pregnant. But I was wrong. In the early hours of the morning he was banging on our bedroom door asking to be let in, to come and join him for a drink. I had to put a chair up against the door to prevent him coming in. I sat there most of the night. The next day we got a lift into the university and went to Charles Lemert, a sociologist with whom I had made contact, and pleaded with him to give us shelter. He did, and he and his wife Bonnie took us in, arranged a lift back to New York, and persuaded us to come back to study: Aileen to do a Masters in Fine Art and I to do a PhD in Sociology.

When we came back the following August, Carbondale was like an oasis of sex, full of hot, voluptuous young women. Sex was like hunting. Anyone could be a predator. The pursuit of sex meant that at a party, even though I was there with Aileen and Arron, a woman would come up to me and look at me, not really listening to what I was saying, and just have a good look. I could feel her undressing me. There was no sense of shame or awkwardness.

I cannot remember her name but I can see her clearly: shoulder length brown hair, tanned face, smooth, svelte body in a green dress. She oozed sex. Aileen and I had arrived earlier at the party. It was an informal pot-luck affair being hosted by her husband. She sidled up to us. After a while, Aileen went off with Arron, and we were left talking. She asked me if I liked gardening. I lied. She asked me if I would like to see her roses. I lied again. She led me outside to the back yard, and then around to the back of the garage. There were no roses. There wasn't a flower. She leaned forward and we had a long, sensual kiss that got longer. She pulled her dress down around her waist. I was on a rollercoaster. I was doing fine until she lay down on the grass. I realised that she wanted to go all the way. I recoiled in fear. It was as if I had come to Las Vegas. I wanted to gamble, but I couldn't take the chance.

I try to see myself that Sunday afternoon, the wannabe cool Irish dude, befuddled and confused. What was is that she saw in me? Was it my voice? Aileen always said it was one of the things that attracted her. Did she see me as something exotic? Did she do this with everyone and anyone? I tried to persuade myself that I had behaved responsibly, that I had stood by Aileen when I was tempted by this beautiful sexual viper. Why did I not just jump in? What was I afraid of? Was it that Aileen would find out and that it would cause a crisis from which our marriage may not have recovered? Was I afraid that it would open the floodgates? Was this another example of a shy, awkward Catholic man being sexually out of his depth? Or was it more about some age-old moral imperative working through me. I could fantasise about having sex with beautiful women. I could imagine what it would be like: the sight, smell and feel of a hot, voluptuous body, a beautiful woman offering herself to me. But when it happened in real life and she was there on a plate in front of me, I froze. Maybe I was shocked by a woman behaving like a man. We went back into the party, and she behaved as if nothing had happened. I asked her if she would like to meet up again and she said no, it was just one of those spontaneous things.

I was caught in no man's land, between wanting to explore new realms of flesh and yet hold on to Aileen. It was as if Carbondale was a sexual laboratory. People came with the intention of experimenting. When it came to balancing lust and love, the scales seemed heavily tipped towards lust. Carbondale was like many other American universities: it was a place of self-discovery away from home. It was a place where sex, drugs, pleasure and self-interest could be fulfilled. It was a retreat house from reality where students pursued the American dream before entering the real world of emotional upheaval, conflict, separation, divorce and depression.

It was evident in their bodies. The women sauntered slowly around the campus in their tanned skin, laden down with sex and beauty. I was amazed, not just at the difference in their bodies, but at the way they walked and held themselves. They lolled about the place like big gorillas languishing in the heat of the jungle. It was August, and the humidity and the temperature were both close to 100 degrees. They talked liked they walked, with a long Southern drawl. I wondered what made them so free and randy. In the beginning I thought it was all the dope they smoked. They were so laid back that they seemed to fall into sex as if they were sliding into a warm bath. And for some, gender did not seem to make that much difference.

After a year, we seemed to spend more time hanging out and partying with people in the fine art programme than with sociologists. Mike, one of the sculptors, took a fancy to Aileen. He was a very good-looking guy. As we were more house-bound with Arron, who was around a year old at the time, he used to come over to dinner quite often. He made no bones about his attraction to Aileen and, eventually, one night he came on to her too strong. Aileen told him that she had had enough, and went off to bed. I was wondering if I should ask him to leave. I felt a bit sorry for him. He should have known that Irish flirts never go all the way. We had another beer and he kindly offered to help me clear up and do the dishes. I was at the sink, with my back turned, washing and talking when he tapped me on the shoulder. As I turned he held my head and plunged his tongue into my mouth. I pushed him away. I had not seen this coming. Was I blind? As I fumbled about the kitchen, I asked him what had brought that on. He looked at me and asked if I had not realised that his advances towards Aileen were only a ruse to get to me.

Mike was good at spontaneously pursing happiness. The following year he met Susan and, after a few months, they decided they were going to get married. Having gotten married in a rush myself, I was sympathetic to all this. But they were talking about next week. They would have to go to the next town but there were logistical problems. They needed two witnesses, and Mike asked if Aileen and I would be willing to go along. The problem was that the only available time was the following Wednesday at 11.00. We told him we were free but there were other complications. Susan had classes at 9.00 and 12.00 which she did not want to skip. This meant that any celebration would have to be postponed until that evening. A year later they split up, and Susan went to another university.

The culture of dope and sex was very different to the one of drink and sex back home. Among the more mature graduates, there was moral aversion to alcohol. It was a strange world for Aileen and me. It was never anything other than home-grown grass, and people took pride in their crop. If people did drink alcohol, it was nothing more than a couple of cans of beer or a glass of wine. It did not take much time to realise how hung up they could be about drink. When Aileen and I went to one of our first pot-luck barbeques, we brought a bottle of gin, cans of tonic and lots of lemons. Being able to buy a bottle of gin was a real treat for us: it was about a quarter of the cost at home. I went around offering to make people a gin and tonic, but everyone said they were happy with their cans of beer and soda. It was completely different when a joint was being passed round. Besides the usual sucking and inhaling, there was a closing of the eyes, and then the complimentary words of praise, as if they had been tasting some fine wine. It was a strange religious ritual; a different way of achieving collective effervescence. Bringing in the gin was an act of profanity. When we were leaving, the hostess came up to me and, holding the half full bottle with the ends of her fingers with the same look of disdain as if it was a dirty nappy we had left on the sofa, she asked me if I would like to take it home with me. 'We don't keep liquor in our house,' she said.

My naivety eventually caught up with me. In the first lecture course I gave I was really taken aback by the standard, not so much of what they knew but of their writing. I had required them to write an essay, but they were used to short exam answers or ticking boxes on multiple choice questions. One student in particular was devastated that I had given her essay a D-. In reality the mark was very generous. The essay was a complete failure: three pages of big, clumsy handwriting with not one grammatically correct sentence. She stayed behind after class. She was a stunning black girl. She said she was desperate to do well and asked me if I could give her some advice. She asked if I had time to go over her essay. She suggested going for a coffee. In the canteen, I was pointing out her mistakes when she leaned over and asked if there was anything more she could do to get a better grade. I went red with embarrassment and told her that I hoped she was not suggesting what I thought she was. I got up immediately and left. I stopped off in the library to get some books, and by the time I got back to the department, Gerry Gaston, the Head, called me in to tell me that the student had filed a complaint against me with Affirmative Action.

'You'll be fine,' he said. 'Just play the Irish sexual innocence card.'

Aileen had finished her degree by Christmas 1982, and we went to live in Jersey City for six months. We hoped to work and save enough to do a grand tour over to the West coast and back. However, I had been central to the organisation of a social ecology conference at the university, which meant that I had to go back down to Carbondale for a few days. I drove down with Wayne, a good friend from Jersey. We decided that we would wait and see if we were offered a place to stay and, if not, find a cheap motel. We were in luck. Karen, one of the students helping to organise the conference, said that the students with whom she rented a house were away and there was plenty of room. The next day we were walking through the university. It was a quiet Saturday during Spring break. She said she needed to stop by her room to get something. I was no longer naïve and figured she might be up to something; she had tried to hold my hand as we walked back from coffee. I suspected that there was more to going to her room than to collect a book. I was prepared for any assault. But I was not prepared for the makeshift bed that she had in her room. Rooms were strictly for working and studying only. It was forbidden to stay overnight. Karen told me they rarely checked, and it was easier some nights to stay over rather than drive all the way home. She was reassuring but I was too nervous. My desire was quelled by my fears: there were too many what ifs. That night, as I was still going over the 'what ifs', she came to my room. It was a brief and rather uneventful exercise.

Why did I let myself go with Karen? I was like a young boy left alone in a sweetshop, overwhelmed by the array of goodies on offer and by the ease with which I could pick and choose. And yet, when it came to choosing, I didn't. I just took that which was offered to me. Maybe it was because I was away from home. I could have a fling without causing any hurt to Karen and Aileen. I could have free sex without feeling guilty.

The reality was that I was still a Catholic at heart. I could not contain my guilt. I told Aileen about Karen almost immediately after I arrived home. She was disappointed but phlegmatic. She was hurt, but accepted that it was a once-off and soon put it behind her. Aileen may have had a huge sexual appetite, but she was also enormously sexually jealous.

But telling Aileen was not sufficient, I felt compelled to confess myself to my mother and wrote to her the following week. She was confused, and told me that there was too much detail. I also felt the need to ensure that Karen was not hurt and so wrote to her.

This confused her and she wanted to explore my motivations in writing. After the exchange of some letters, I realised that a fling was turning into an emotional affair. I talked to Aileen, and she suggested it would be a good idea to stop writing.

I learnt as much about myself and the differences between love and sex in those years as I did about sociology. It is easy to fall into sex, and in many ways 'falling in love' is often about falling into sex. But having sex is different from making love: no matter how much sexual stimulation there may be, it is difficult to stay aroused. And although there was a free and easy approach to sex in Carbondale, I never thought that I was immersed in a highly erotic sexual culture. There seemed to be little nuance. It was like fast food. You picked it up when it was on offer. There was little coyness or coquettishness. And yet America did bring us onto another level. When I went back to Carbondale in 1984 to finish my PhD, in a series of letters we explored our longings and desires and how to deal with these when we were separated. Letter writing became a way of reflecting on our relationship, our attraction, weaknesses and temptations. This was one of the letters that she wrote, some years later when she went back to the States.

> *Sexually speaking dear man I have been completely celibate, no masturbating which is unusual for me over such a long period of time. Sometimes it seems highly distasteful, others it's just a physical release that it suspends such an attitude. When I was pregnant with all our three*

children, I certainly masturbated every day we didn't make love. I always felt like a big erotic zone, a fecund whore/mother being. It wasn't a problem. I liked being that way. I imagine it was partly the hormonal and physical changes. I always preferred Renoir's full fleshy sensuous women to Tom Wolfe's 'x-rays' his wonderful description of the socialite who continually starves to maintain a svelte like figure. When I use the term 'distasteful' it's not that I disapprove at all, it's just as you say empty, I need a man to satisfy me, that self absorption is way off what I need. Maybe it's because I'm so consumed with self in relation to work that more in relation to sexual relief would be totally undesirable. Being pregnant, no man could have physically satisfied me all the time so the mixture was great as it is normally although with less frequency. So I rather work out hard and play back the sexual drives, in fact focus them all towards being with you again. I have and play with desire and attraction, you know a softening towards someone that you suspect could be interesting or even more a type of blind animal sexual high that some people rise in you. Maybe I'm writing into intensity that passes the more gentle flicker of normality. You know all the body language that reveals attraction that is such a part of human relations we often don't even consciously mark it. I think I might probably have had many relationships if I hadn't met you so young. I think I could have easily have swung into a sexual appetite of difference. I liked me a lot more when I was younger but somehow with the passing of time the sum of their parts rarely matches those women I have come to know. How did I find you? I know you'd be pragmatic and reel out some sociological logic, but I don't want to hear that. We have such a good sexual play between us and being with you makes me feel so whole that it's maybe a form of passion when sexual jealousy fires me. Maybe that's also something that diminishes with age, getting beyond the infantile possessiveness and fear of rejection. I understand a lot more, reading Jung and Freud helped, and recognising my emotional inheritance from Dad. And I miss you now. I was toying with the idea of going home midterm next week. But I think it wouldn't be wise emotionally or financially. I have a huge longing to be with you again which moves through many emotions. I love you man and wish I was in your arms now. Hold, hug and kiss Olwen and Arron for me. Aileen.

14

I think of all the time we made love and I think of her dying where I am lying. In the brief history of time, our lives together seem to have transcended death. Yet there is a fine line between life and death. Sometimes I think I am nothing more than a misguided mayfly, fooled by belief and meaning into thinking that just because I last longer I am some higher being. The mayfly lives in tune with a wider whole of which it is part. I live in nature but I am not part of it. It is only when I saw Aileen in such pain, terrified by death but unable to say a word, that I realised that at the end, when all meaning has gone out the door, that we return to nature and die as animals. In between time we live the delusion that we are masters of the universe, morally superior to nature and all other species. Sometimes, in these moments of lying and being, I become still and get a feeling of being beyond here. It is the same sensation I often got after we made love. It could be an affinity with nature, with animal being. It is during moments of birth and death that I have gained glimpses of another way of being and feeling.

I sink back into the material world of coming and going, mastering and controlling, achieving and regulating, getting and spending, and it is lost. The more I try to rationalise and control death, to overcome it and nail it down, to say what it is, the less I understand it. The mayfly is not beset by its death, by the meaning of life. Mayflies do not have the ability to create and store meaning, to develop large, shared deposits of emotional experiences, to be able to rummage in their memories, delving into the sensory etchings left on the brains and bodies. And yet there was an impulse and an instinct, within both Aileen and I, to go on living and breeding because we were going to die.

It was strange, having gone through all the earlier years of living in fear of pregnancy that we should set out to have a child deliberately. Aileen had discovered some small lumps in her breast. She was very anxious until the doctor confidently announced that they were milk solids and the best way of getting rid of them was to have a child and breast-feed.

I learned quite a bit about myself and about the emotional and psychic distance between Aileen and I during that pregnancy. I may have become a reasonably good lover and husband, but I felt out of my depth when it came to pregnancy. As with almost everything she did, Aileen devoted herself to being pregnant, reading books, exercising and dieting. As I read a book or the newspaper, she would read out passages from her *Well Woman* book about what stage the baby was at, signs and symptoms she should look out for. She might have got more response if she read out some sport results. Yes, I touched the bump, felt the feet movements in her womb, listened to the heartbeat and engaged in the practice of being a devoted, caring husband who lifted heavy things and who said nice, supportive things. In reality, I was physically and emotionally detached.

In many respects we were a picture postcard couple. We prepared for the baby's arrival, I went to her consultations with the gynaecologist and we practised the Lamaze method together. This was, after all, what cool, new, liberated men did. I felt proud and morally responsible. I could rattle off knowledge that I had learnt from Aileen about pregnancy and impress not just my male friends but, because Aileen was one of the first of our generation to give birth, some of our female friends too. But much of it was empty role play. I was not really concerned let lone engaged in the pregnancy. I had no understanding of how it dominated her everyday life, how the baby took over her body, how vulnerable she felt. My main anxiety was that everything would work out. I was fearful that I would lose her.

Arron was born in 1979. There were complications after. Aileen became very ill. At first it was put down to post-natal depression, but then she began to lose weight and, eventually, started fainting. She was rushed to hospital where the next day they removed a cyst the size of a golf ball from one of her ovaries. There were also cultural complications. The revolution against the Church was gaining momentum and Aileen and I had told our parents that we were not going to get Arron baptised. My brother, Maurice, was incensed. The previous Christmas morning we had a chat. We were in the garage in Ardtona: he was supposed to be at Mass and he had asked me to come and have a drink and idle away the time. He took the opportunity to grasp the baptism nettle. As he sipped his whiskey, he stopped and looked at me.

'You know you can't go ahead with this.'

'What?'

'Not getting the baby baptised.'

'Why?'

'It will break Mum's heart.'

'Jaysus, Maurice, when will the hypocrisy stop?'

'Please, just not now. It will spoil everything.'

'But don't you see the ludicrousness of it all?'

'Ah yes,' he said. 'But Mum is not ludicrous.'

Aileen became pregnant again in 1985. It was all part of our great family plan: when I had finished my PhD in 1984, we decided we would have two more children quite close in age to each other. She was about three months pregnant. I remember her anxiety about getting past the twelfth week and the relief that came with having reached that milestone. We were on our way down to Brittas Bay. It was a Sunday morning. She said she was not feeling well so we called into the Wicklow Arms, and while I sat with Arron in the reception area and read the paper, she went to the toilet. She came back and said she had passed a lot of blood. I was concerned but I was also wondering if this spelt the end of our holiday. Was she being overly concerned? 'How much blood?' I asked. What was I thinking? She was worried and confused. She phoned her mother. We decided to go on. But by the time we got to the caravan, we realised that it was something more serious than a bleed. We drove back to Dublin and went straight to Mount Carmel hospital. They did what they could, but she miscarried the following morning. She was devastated. She had already developed a relationship with the foetus. Before the procedure, she asked them to keep the foetus so that she could see it. She told me about the little head, hands and feet.

I was taken aback by how physically and emotionally overwhelmed Aileen was by the experience. She was grieving. I began to think that I was to blame. I had little or no understanding of miscarriages. If I was not so ignorant maybe I might have insisted on returning to Dublin immediately. Maybe the baby could have been saved. Maybe I was just plain selfish and did not want a little blood to spoil my day at the seaside. Maybe I was relieved that it was the baby and not Aileen that had died. I was bewildered by her distress. The reality is that I had not formed any relationship with the foetus. I did not conceive of it becoming a baby that would grow to have a life of its own. I had no real sense of attachment and so no real sense of loss.

Aileen learnt a hard lesson that in Ireland, in 1985, miscarriage was a very private, personal matter. It was not something that was discussed, even among women. Miscarriage, like the menopause, was hidden away. They were women's issues; they were not part of 'good' society. But, like many other things, the Irish were late with any public recognition and awareness of women's private troubles. Irish women came from a long line of mothers who had become used to being pregnant, to having miscarriages, to seeing their children die young, or watching them grow up and emigrate never to be seen again. They were used to being shunned and silenced by men who were frightened and disgusted by bleeding women.

In 1986, she became pregnant again. We were delighted. Our grand plan was back on track. Everything went smoothly this time, and Luke was born in February 1987. It was an exciting time. We both had good jobs. Aileen had a full-time post as a lecturer in fine art in the National College of Art. I had a temporary post in UCD. We had moved to our big, new, beautiful house in Rathgar. We were well off. We were deeply embedded in a dense network of family and friends. We were cruising.

It was towards the end of Thursday's lecture in UCD when Pat Clancy opened the door and came down the stairs. It was usual for lecturers, at the end of the lecture, to make an announcement. Students had begun to gather round to ask questions, but I was distracted by the way he was coming down the steps. I knew, without him saying anything, that there was something wrong. There was no reassuring smile. I thought it must be Mum. I didn't hear the questions any more. I was completely focused on Pat. Then he told me: there had been an accident at home and Luke had been taken to hospital. He drove me to Our Lady's Hospital for Sick Children in Crumlin. And all the time we were chatting, and all the time he was reassuring me, but my mind was spinning.

That day had begun like many other days. I had gotten up, as usual for a weekday, about half past six. I went downstairs and heated the bottle that had been prepared the night before. I brought it up to Aileen and brought Luke in to her. I went into Arron's room, wakened him, and led him sleepily back into my side of the bed. I left to take Frodo the dog for a walk.

When I came back from the walk I made the breakfast. As usual, about a quarter to eight, I began to hear the sounds of the descent down the stairs. There was the little ritual on the top landing, at the window overlooking the back garden. They would stop to inspect the day. Luke would try to reach out and eat it. Arron would leap down the last few flights of stairs and Luke would cry out in delight.

After the grand entry to the kitchen, we all settled down to eat, listen to the radio, read the paper. Luke sat in his high chair between Aileen and I. He sucked on some crusts of bread. When he became bored with this, he casually leaned over the edge of his chair and dropped a crust onto the floor where Frodo sat and waited.

Aileen and Arron went upstairs to do his homework. Luke and I stayed on in the kitchen. I fed him and while he played with Frodo I did the dishes. About a quarter past eight, I brought him upstairs. As I came round the top of the stairs, Aileen had just reached the living room door. She smiled. Luke, like myself, was a sucker for her smile. As I held his outstretched hands, he eagerly moved his feet towards her. He was learning to walk. We were convinced that he would be walking by Christmas, or certainly by his first birthday in February.

I made the sandwiches and packed the lunches. I went upstairs and played with Luke until the doorbell rang. When he heard it, Luke became uneasy and quiet. He sensed that our babysitter Pauline had arrived and that soon we would all be gone and he would not see us again until late in the afternoon. His precious morning was coming to an end. He had hopes and wishes. He cried loud and hard. He broke our hearts.

About the same time that I began to give my lecture, Pauline went up to change Luke's nappy. As she came back down, and was about six steps from the bottom, Luke stretched forward. Maybe he was trying to imitate the way Arron jumped down the last few steps, maybe he wanted to get to Frodo more quickly. Maybe he hoped that there was a surprise downstairs, that we had not gone out, and that we were all in the kitchen waiting for him. Whatever thoughts were going through his mind, he did not realise that they would be some of his last. Whatever hopes he had about what the day would bring, he did not realise he had no hope. He jerked forward. It was enough to unbalance Pauline. As she reached to the banister to steady herself, Luke tumbled from her right arm down the stairs. As he careered through space everything in his life depended on how he was going to land on the concrete floor below. We used to call him Lucky Luke. He had no luck that morning. He landed on the back of his head. If only he had twisted just a tiny bit, he might have landed on his face or on his side.

As soon as I arrived into the hospital, one of the doctors took me into a small room and told me that although they knew that he had fallen down the stairs, they could find nothing wrong. He was, however, very weak. They strongly suspected that he had a virulent form of meningitis which could have done untold damage if they had not caught it in time. 'In a way,' he said, 'it was fortunate that he had the fall.' The reason for them thinking it was meningitis was that there was a slight rash on his forearm and the fact that there had been four cases earlier that week.

Aileen arrived. All I could do was to look into her eyes and she knew and she screamed. We wailed there in the entrance to the hospital. Shortly afterwards we were allowed to go in to see him. He was so still. His breathing was heavy and awkward. He was fighting for his life. It was later that afternoon that the doctors became aware of the swelling at the back of his head. They decided that the head injury was worse than they had originally thought and that the bleeding was from his brain. He was transferred to Richmond hospital for a CT scan. The doctor there told us that he had a heavy fracture but that there was no sign of clotting. We were still hopeful. I think the doctor was holding back on the truth. When we got back to Crumlin another doctor told us he had lost half of his blood into the back of his head.

Aileen and I decided to stay the night in the waiting room. One of the nurses got us pillows and blankets and folded down the couch for us. In the middle of the night, one of the doctors came in to tell us that he was holding his own. That was the last message of hope. At 6.00 a.m. I went in to see him. I knew then for certain that he was going to die, even though he looked as beautiful as ever, so serene, so calm, breathing easily with the respirator. But it was a false breath. Take away the life support and he would die.

And every time we went into that little intensive care room, I cried from the depths of my being. I had never known anything that had torn me apart so completely. There was no possibility of being brave. I would hold back the tears for a few seconds, and then the enormity of what confronted me would crash in like a tidal wave. There was nothing that could be done now. We awaited the results of the brain scan. It confirmed that there was no activity. He was brain dead. Now we could tell ourselves and the rest of the world.

We arranged to go back to the hospital the following morning to say our last farewell. We had decided the previous evening to donate his organs. There was to be a big operation that afternoon: the medics and the nurses were very excited. Organ transplant operations were still relatively rare. A little girl in the hospital was waiting for his liver. One of his kidneys was going to England, the other to Austria. We went in and took our last photographs. The nurses were able to take him off the ventilator very briefly so that we could each hold him in our arms for one last moment.

We waited for the leading surgeon to arrive to sign the necessary papers. He was half an hour late. When he eventually arrived, he announced that there was no need to sign any papers. I was furious. He became a scapegoat for my anger. I asked him what would happen if, in three months time, I was to turn around and say that we never signed off on the donations? Another surgeon decided that it would be a good idea for us to sign something. So he got Luke's chart and at the end of the first page, wrote something like: 'We, Tom Inglis and Aileen MacKeogh, consent to the donation of our son Luke's organs…' We signed, but it left a foul feeling.

The decision to donate his organs may have been noble, and probably the correct thing to do, but I am not sure if I would do it again. There was a gung-ho attitude at the time of using every opportunity to practice this new medicine. Luke may have been brain dead – I accept that – but does that mean that he did not feel anything as they took out his organs? When does life begin? At birth? At the moment of conception? And when does it end? The thoughts of those final hours have haunted me. Did we make the right decision? It was one of the few things that I could not talk to Aileen about. It may have been the correct decision, but it tainted our grief.

Sadly, the transplant operation was to no avail. When we went in to see him the following morning, the little girl who had been waiting for his liver lay beside him. She had died during the operation. He was in his blue pyjamas, all zipped up so that only his head was showing. I could only imagine the inside story, the horrific scars left after the plunder. He looked pale, but still peaceful and serene. I touched his hand. It was cold, icy cold. We left Arron's favourite teddy bear beside him. He had given it to Luke for his last journey.

When we took Luke from the mortuary on the Monday evening, we put his little white coffin in the back of our Morris Minor and drove ourselves out to Kilmacanogue where he was to be buried in the grave that Aileen's parents had organised for themselves. On that poignant journey through Enniskerry and on up the back road to Kilmacanogue we went up the little road that brings you to the top of the Rocky Valley. It was already dark; it was the end of November. We sat in silence looking across the valley to Powerscourt and beyond. It was a clear night and the stars were already twinkling. Aileen said 'I hope he is up there somewhere.'

Aileen and I never lost touch with each other during that time. We kept close all the time. We sat, slept, cried and walked together. We looked out for each other. Sometimes I would come across her and I would know from her demeanour that she was very low. I would hug her tightly. When you lose something really precious, you want to hold on so strongly to what you have left. It was beautiful. We made passionate love in those days. It seemed the obvious response to death and the meaninglessness of life.

15

My sense of loss after Luke died was different. We had developed a bond that was beyond words. I often wonder what was going on in his mind. He was at that stage of discovery, of exploring the world, becoming independent, and yet still completely dependent. My memories are of holding him, hugging and caring for him. In the years after his death, Aileen and I traced back all the events of his short life. She compiled an album of photographs. For years I carried his little red glove that had fallen from his hand the previous Sunday when we walked around the gardens of Powerscourt. It was in the pocket of the overcoat that Aileen had made for me during the Christmas of 1975. I would forget it was there until I reached in and felt it.

For years, I pondered – what if? What if he had not been so bloody minded as to arch his back and try to struggle out of Pauline's arms that moment? What if he had landed on any other part of his head? What if the doctors had seen the bleeding in his brain sooner? What if he had lived, what would he be like now? What difference would it have made to Aileen and I? It was one small move among millions of other possible moves that sent our lives down completely different tracks.

Although we talked and remembered Luke, grief is profoundly personal. I like to think Aileen's breast cancer was linked to losing Luke, that her breast was the centre of her nurturing, and that the cancer was a reaction to the loss of Luke. She told me that she had read that there was some definite evidence, but I checked and there isn't. It is a nice myth.

I look back now at those years after Luke died and see them differently. I see her grief through a different lens, through my grieving for her. Grief can inspire as much as overwhelm you. There is a realisation, not just of how fragile and unfair life can be, but of the privilege to be alive and well. Death enhances the imperative to squeeze as much as you can from life, to indulge in its pleasures, to make the world a better place.

It had been obvious for some time that Aileen had been struggling with her work as a lecturer in the National College of Art. She was finding the atmosphere unbearable. She had ideas and plans, but they were being continually thwarted by an old guard that did not want change. More importantly perhaps, she was struggling with her art work. She had not been able to get back into her studio. She could not find any inspiration to be creative. Luke's death not only challenged the meaning of her life, it seemed to make the pursuit of art pointless.

For Aileen, art was more than the creation of beautiful objects, it was about challenging the way we read and understand the world. It is about trying to get people to see things differently, to stir the imagination. It has to be attractive and stimulating. It needs to be rewarding to look at. It is helpful, but not necessary, that it is visually appealing. Good art makes you stop, look and reflect. Aileen was concerned with challenging perception and understanding, but also about making the environments in which she lived beautiful. She had no difficulty in expressing herself with colour and design. She had enormous self-confidence. It seemed to ooze out of her. Neither of her parents was artistic: there was little or no art in the house and there were no artistic heroes in the immediate family. But she was one of the new confident suburban bourgeoisie that emerged in Ireland in the 1960s. She was a product of her class. She had her own bedroom, her own fields and private forest. She had the freedom, time and space to retreat from the world, to play and make believe. Over the years, when I would come upon Aileen making art, she seemed to be in a different world, between transfixion and transcendence, totally immersed. It was as if she had entered another realm of being. She was in the world, but not of it. She was ethereal. In this world, she worked with a host of different materials and methods, creating drawings, sculptures, shapes and forms.

She had always been concerned with themes of nature, landscapes and trees, the interactions between humans and nature. She wanted to capture the way we shape and dominate nature. She felt that our lack of identity, concern or sympathy for trees was a symptom of our alienation from nature. We do not live with trees. We do not embrace their beauty. We see them more as a means towards ends, for furniture, floors, poles or simply burning.

One of her sculptures that I like is a large wooden square frame of about 7x6 feet into which she placed a number of strong young trees of different shapes and hues. Then, having forced them into her frame, having cut them off in their prime and stuck them into this aesthetic space, she felt sorry for them, and so she set about trying to heal the trees by putting plaster and bandages on the broken limbs, as if they had been in some dreadful machine accident. She called this piece 'Wounded Wood'.

She became concerned about the way humans shape and mould the landscape to their own needs and interests, creating fields, making boundaries, putting a new structure on the surface of the earth. And yet this land had existed for thousands of years; it had its own history that lay beneath the surface, moulded by forces far greater than humans. When we look at fields we are not able to see the nature of this human intervention – to see and recognise the long-term history of the field and the landscape. It is about re-imagining landscape, capturing its shape and form, but also the way humans intervene in the landscape, sometimes physically, and in the way it is perceived and experienced. Everything we see in nature is ours; it exists in the way it is seen and moulded by humans.

When Luke died, these ongoing issues and themes no longer held the same meaning and significance. She had to respond to the raw reality of death and loss. Art for Aileen was never an external, objective, formal activity. It emerged from deep down inside her. As much as she felt the landscape had a history that could be revealed, so too she thought that the task of art was not to exclude the artist, but to very much include her, to make her central to the process.

She produced a drawing of a house. It seemed to me prosaic. It did not have any of the energy and visionary challenge of her landscape pieces. She was dismayed. She was running aground. She needed to withdraw from the world for a time. She came up with the idea of going to Princeton for a semester in the Autumn of 1990. I was a bit taken aback. Olwen had been born less than a year after Luke died. She was just one and half years old. Aileen, however, was determined, so she arranged for a Spanish au-pair to come in, set her up in my study, and headed off to New Jersey for five months.

I was a confused bundle of emotions. I was trying to be supportive, but what was this drive to do her art, this need to be away from me when I needed her so much? She was not there for Olwen's second birthday. She was not there for Luke's third anniversary. Yet I knew she was with me. She explained her need for time and space in one of her letters:

> *Losing Luke disturbed a huge physical and emotional security. I didn't want any more change. I wanted to hold on to things the way they were. And memories of Luke were immediate and somehow physically stored in the walls of our house. Maybe I was emotionally entombing myself in with him in our house. How startling that sentence is in relation to my work. Even as I write the tears roll down for him. Perhaps writing it over dramatises it but I think now, the quiet precious moments allow it to surface, let you at*

that inner core of being. I knew this issue of change, your needs and my position were serious challenges I had to confront on my own.

It was in Princeton that the series of sculptures and drawings that formed the basis of her exhibition *House* began to emerge. Instead of trying to capture the history that lay beneath the land, she set about trying to capture the feelings of grief and loss that lay deep inside her. She was trying to bring to the surface the feelings of fragility and insecurity that permeate our lives. Our houses may seem strong and solid, but houses become homes, and homes are very vulnerable. Homes are built on feelings and emotions. In the sculptures that accompanied the drawings, Aileen explored the way in which we transform bare rooms and walls into places full of beauty and meaning. We pour ourselves into our homes. They become sanctuaries, places of comfort and consolation into which we can escape. Within the interior of our homes we explore the interiors of our lives. We take off the masks we wear outside. We love and care. We pour out our hearts.

How could something as strong and durable as our house and home be so easily shattered? No matter how strong the foundations, no matter how sturdy the walls, nothing could protect the house from a bolt out of the blue, from death. All that was solid melted into air. What rose magnificent and strong from the ground was so easily knocked over. Our safe cocoon, our haven from a heartless world, our warm nest, was but a house of cards.

> *Yesterday I spent working most of the day. In fact, after your call I felt so good that I did a drawing. I felt from the outset it would be good just because of the frame of mind I was in. I wanted to draw a house that exuded an inner strength under a dark and foreboding shell. I don't know if you remember last February I told you I did a drawing for your birthday. I can't rightly remember how I got the feeling you weren't too impressed by it. But it was a special drawing to me, I wanted the house to convey how precious you and our lives together, our family, our home, is amidst all else around us, in fact the only drawing that I immediately titled emerged from that desire 'Glowing House'. I think of it as your drawing. I think the same emotions stirred yesterday's work.*

But the *House* work was really all about Luke. It was about the pain and sense of loss that welled up in Aileen after he died. She had been devastated by her miscarriage. But his death was overwhelming. It took two years before the rawness of the pain began to ease and she was able to start working on her art again.

She was able to harness the experience of grief and, using her artistic creativity, find a way not just of expressing that pain but of saying something deeply significant about our lives, the spaces in which we live, and the way in which we create meaning and beauty. It would be wrong to think that Aileen's grief was a means to being artful, or that her art was a means of grieving. In creating something artistic, she was able to deal with loss. Out of loss came creation. Art is an almost unconscious reaction to life and death, to the beauty and terror of our existence, to the order and chaos that lie beneath the surface.

Soon after *House*, she began working with flowers. At first she explored the meaning of flowers, the way that certain flowers came to symbolise different sentiments. Later she moved quite dramatically to squeezing flowers to death. In *Deadheading*, another installation piece, she constructed her own flower presses, free-standing on tall legs. She took flowers at their prime. She chose ones with long stems – tulips and irises. She put them into the presses, and turned the screws until the two glass plates had come together and crushed the head of the flower, leaving the long stem adrift. She wanted to explore the conflicting emotions evoked by confronting life, death and beauty. Each day she would take photos of the flowers as life was slowly squeezed out of them. Shortly after she undertook this series of work, she was diagnosed with the cancer which eventually, slowly but surely, squeezed the life out of her.

Throughout her illness, Aileen was always phlegmatic about her potential death. It was reflected in a piece she wrote for the catalogue that accompanied her flower installation:

> *From the very beginning of our lives the only certainty is that we will die. Yet there is an unnatural fear of death. We are happy to look at life. We take delight in documenting its various manifestations. But we are uncomfortable in looking death in the eye. We are even more*

uncomfortable looking at something beautiful dying. There is a time and place for death and everything should be in its proper time and place.

And if there is a time for death, so too is there a time for life, a time for beauty. Aileen had this enormous compulsion, an aesthetic imperative that became moral, to make life beautiful. It was an ongoing project. She was always thinking visually. How could she make the space she was in more beautiful? How could she combine colour and light to create a pleasurable environment? I learnt a lot from her, but I am not committed to beauty in the same way. She used to berate me regularly for not attending to the spaces in which I lived. Most of the time, she undertook this task herself, even when it was more my own private space, like the study at home or my room in college. She thought I was lazy about my living environment. She regularly gave out to me about lighting. She said that the ambiance of a beautiful room was lost without proper lighting.

I still live in the beauty that she created. As you come in through the yellow hall door, her *Wounded Wood* dominates the hall. There are other artists' work on the walls, but your eye is drawn to the stained glass windows that Aileen made overlooking the stairs down to the kitchen. The two living rooms are full of sculptures from her series: *Land Lesions*. The walls and ceilings are painted in a mixture of dark and light blue, the carpet is light bluish grey, and the couches and chairs are big, soft and white. It is a cocoon. The stairs down the kitchen are a constant reminder of the fragility of life, and there is a drawing from the *House* series opposite where Luke fell and another in the kitchen.

There are a pair of glass doors in the kitchen that lead out onto the patio. The path to the left of the pond is surrounded by an Azalea, a Star Magnolia, a Copper Beach, rose bushes and lilies. The pond is surrounded by ornate pots. The archway into the second half of the garden is covered with Honeysuckle. The path is bordered on the right by a raised lawn and to the left by Fuchsia, Berberis, Acer and, in season, Alliums and Peony Roses. At the end of the path, there is an enormous black bamboo that hangs over the tall window that lets the light into her studio.

What was this relentless pursuit of beauty, this never ending quest to make the space in which she lived more beautiful? Shortly before she died, Aileen turned to me. She was propped up in bed; I was reading the paper. She was looking out across the rooftops of Winton Avenue. She stopped and looked over at me intently.

'I hope people will not think that I was arrogant the way I pursued beauty.'

'No, of course not,' I said.

But I never asked her what she meant or why she should have thought like that.

When she was diagnosed with breast cancer, the surgeon cut off one of her breasts and the chemo took her hair away. Now, instead of her home, her own body was under attack. Again she turned to art to understand, explore and capture this experience. She knew how much I hated to see her body ravaged by the disease, but she was determined to document it. She wanted to take photos of her hairless, breastless body, mainly as a basis for doing drawings. She knew that it would be too much to ask me, so she asked Arron. He obliged. The photos were harrowing. There is something raw and humiliating when you see a photo of a bald woman with huge scars where her breast had been. When you strip off the clothes, you are left with the nakedness and suffering of human being. Aileen wanted to confront her frailty and mortality. Instead of trying to hide away from cancer, to refer to it obliquely in hushed tones, she wanted to confront it, to bare all.

She went one step further. Part of the confrontation would be to take a photo of herself in a coffin. She phoned up a number of undertakers. Eventually one agreed to her proposal. She was told to come at lunchtime. She went with her sister, Carol. The idea was that Carol would take the photos. The undertaker showed them into his display room. He had put a coffin down on the floor. He left. But there was a problem. There was no lock on the door. So while Aileen stripped naked, Carol stood at the door keeping watch. She had difficulty trying to get the right shot, holding the camera up above her. She told me afterwards that she was not pleased with them: she could only get from her shoulders down, and even then they were not good. I never saw them.

16

It is difficult to get a clear picture of those years after Luke died. I think that sharing such an amazing experience brought us closer together, as it had done during our time in Yugoslavia. I became more attached to Aileen. I could not bear to let her go. I could not bear when she went away. But we did move on. Aileen was never one for taking to the bed. But it is as easy to be overwhelmed by grief as to be caught up in the illusion of life, to be consumed by its pleasures, discomforts and petty concerns. You might think I would have learnt from Luke's death and be able to transcend these limitations, to live a life of calmness without distractions and the emotional upheavals that eat away at the possibility of pleasure and happiness. And yet, all so easily and all so quickly, I got sucked back into a way of being, of getting things done, of making things happen, that makes me think I learnt little from little Luke. I wanted to become more detached from the world, to be closer to death, so that if it struck again, I would not be taken by surprise; I would be ready. Sometimes I was amazed at how deeply Luke's death had affected Aileen. At other times, I was shocked at how easily she seemed to be able to immerse herself in the world of organisational life, management, diplomacy, and power struggles. I found it difficult to let her go.

It became a regular occurrence, holding on until she came back. I can see myself. I am standing in the middle of my study. I am looking out through the window into the front garden and the road beyond. I am waiting for her to turn the car in through the gate. It is well past six thirty. She has not phoned. It must mean that she will be coming in any time now. I go back into the kitchen. Dinner is ready; it is just a question of keeping it from spoiling. I come back into the study. I sit down at the computer. I try to read or write. It is no good. I want her to come now, but there is still no sign. I return to the kitchen. It is close to the time of deciding whether to turn things off. It is a final act, not for the food, but for me and my emotions.

My feeling of excitement is turning to a feeling of disappointment. The effervescence of love is no longer bubbling. I slowly become disenchanted and depressed. My heart is aching. I feel destroyed. How can she do this to me? Why? Does she not realise how painful this is? How can she be more attached to her work, to them, the organisational people? The feelings of anger and hate begin to well up. Like devils they have taken over my soul. I try to talk to myself. Why am I being so stupid? But the devils are in ascendance. They seem to mock my attempts to regain control of my emotions, my life, my love.

Then I hear the car coming in. But it is too late. My love has gone sour. It has turned to anger. Instead of getting up and running to the door and sweeping Aileen into my arms and telling her how much I love her, I remain rigid at my desk. I have turned to stone. Aileen probably suspected from the second she turned the key in the door that any hope of a warm, loving welcome was doomed. There was no immediate shout or greeting from the study, no words or exclamations of welcome. When she came into the study she would have known by the fact that I was still sitting at my computer that my emotional condition was worse than she had feared. She could smell the mixture of anger and disappointment. There was no point in approaching me. I had gone beyond touch. I was deep into digging my emotional hole.

She looks at me optimistically. 'Sorry sweetie, the meeting went on and on.' I look up. There is no smile, not the faintest sign of love. I portray a calculated coldness; my words are chosen to have maximum effect. 'If you had an appointment with Bertie Ahern [the then Taoiseach] you would have been on time.' I could see the disappointment on her face. 'Why oh why?' she must have wondered, 'does he have to be like this?' Now I look back and think of the pain that I caused. I can imagine her driving home and hoping that I would not be like she feared, that somehow I would have undergone a transformation, that there would be no distance, that when she entered the house the man she loved would embrace her with love.

No, I insisted on going for the kill. There would be a silence and I would say 'Aileen, if I have told you once, I have told you a hundred times, when you are on your deathbed, you won't be thinking of Dun Laoghaire and they won't be thinking of you.' And I would get up and we would go and eat and it would take minutes, sometimes hours and sometimes a day or more for me to thaw. During that time I would hate her, I would hate myself. I would want to give in, to let go, to go back to where I wanted to be, to be with her again, in tune.

I knew it would end, and what made the hateful distance more appealing was that, when it did, it would be so beautiful. But when I was in the zone of hate, when I was possessed like that, I seemed to take pleasure in hurting her. I wanted to teach her a lesson. She had broken the first commandment: 'Thou shalt be devoted to the one you love, above all else, above all others.'

They were such intense emotions. Going from the expectation of bliss to the hell of anger and despondency and, once having fallen into that pit, not being able to pull out, to rescue myself, to rescue her. I wanted her home. My tantrum turned into passive aggression. My refusal to come out of my study, my silence, my few curt, hurtful words, were all perfect emotional bullets, designed to cause the most pain, leaving no evidence that could be used against me. I was the raging jealous husband.

I was not one for giving in easily. This was, after all, a real war of feelings, of interests and responsibilities. Her day revolved around attending meetings, setting agendas, choreographing discussions, making decisions, identifying strategies, implementing tactics, persuading and cajoling the doubters, teasing and gently mocking the self-righteous. Organisational life is mostly about managing people. It is a poker game with emotions being the cards held under the table. Aileen was a master at emotional management. That is why I had to stand up to her.

Aileen was able to manage many people and many things at one time. They call it 'multi-tasking'. However, the trick is that for most of the people, most of the time, they do not feel that they are being managed. I used to get an inclination of this when she would tell me how she had managed the latest change in the Institute and, as I sat listening, I would think 'is she managing me the way she manages people at work?' And I would ask her, and she would look at me and smile and say something like, 'Oh no sweetie, I could never manage you.' She was lying.

Most of my life with Aileen had become a struggle to find a balance between many things: reason and emotions, work and love, lust and love, meaning and nothingness. It was also a balance between more concrete things like the demands of Arron and Olwen, family and friends, cycling, watching sport, gardening, and looking after the dog. But undoubtedly the pressures of work were the greatest cause of stresses and strains. My ability to make love, to create meaning, has been through balancing commitments to work and family, fulfilling immediate sexual desire and developing lasting, caring relationships, being cautious and reckless, holding on to cherished truths and letting them go. I lust for sex, pure, unadulterated, uncomplicated sex but, at the same time, have always wanted love and affection. I want organisation and control in my life, but I also want to feel free to express my emotions, to love in the middle of the day. The meaning of my life is completely arbitrary: it is bound by the culture and time into which I was born. If I had been born among the Taliban, I would see and understand myself and the world differently. There would be a similar difference if I had been born in Ireland a hundred years ago. And yet it seems to me that the urge to love and be loved, to create meaning and to tell the truth, is central to being human.

Aileen loved working. It made her happy. She could be in the garden, the studio, in her office at work, or in her study. It did not seem to make any difference. I, too, have always liked working. I like reading and writing. I can become lost in a sentence or paragraph, working the words. It is work, but it is also a pleasure. It is a discipline. It is also a privilege. I feel withdrawn when I have not written. It is a form of mental constipation.

At the heart of our struggle to make love was the attempt by each of us to grow and develop without smothering or casting a shadow over the other. It is easy to be seduced by the world of work, by the sense of fulfilment that comes from getting things done, from the honour and respect that comes from doing a good job. On the other hand, it is difficult to make love, to keep passion alive, if you don't want to retreat from the world into the confines of the love nest. There was a time and place for Aileen and I to work, and there was a time and place to withdraw into our cocoon and make love. It was a work-love balance worked out every day.

There was also the attempt to balance our careers. We were lucky that for most of our lives we had jobs we liked that did not necessitate living away from home. I had always wanted to get an academic job in sociology, and eventually got one in UCD in 1991. Aileen left the National College of Art the same year and became Director of Arthouse, a new arts centre specialising in digital media that was part of the development of Temple Bar. This was when and where her management career took off. She went from there to the Institute in Dun Laoghaire to become the Head of thc School of Creative Arts.

We also developed a balance in domestic chores. I did the shopping and most of the cooking, Aileen looked after clothes and cleaning. She also looked after the finances. She was responsible for the big spends, obtaining loans, dealing with the bank. She was forever stretching the bank account to its limit. Sometimes it ran dry. That was when emotions ran high. Aileen had this policy that it was best never to be in credit. She had this notion that bank officials gave you much more attention when you owed them money.

I remember a Friday evening and, as usual, I had just done the weekly shopping in Dundrum and went to the ATM to get money to pay at the checkout. It was a regular routine. Alas, there was no money in the account. I had a trolley full of shopping. I phoned her at work. She asked me not to be so angry, as it would achieve nothing. But I was in the middle of a tantrum and was not going to be so easily managed.

'Okay,' I said. 'I will go home and have a drink. There won't be any dinner because there will be no food. I will relax, but I am never doing the shopping again because I told you so many times before that if ever I went to the banklink to do shopping and there was no money, I would hang up my shopping boots. I am sure you will enjoy doing the shopping in the morning.' I put down the phone without waiting for a reply and drove home waiting for the big storm when she would arrive in.

There was no rhyme or reason to our storms. That evening, I came home and I had my gin and tonic and so, before she arrived in, I had relaxed. My feelings of anger and frustration changed to thoughts of bliss. Instead of playing the frustrated, irate husband, I could do something completely different and play the loving, caring husband. After all it was Friday night. There was too much pleasure to be lost in having a row. So I went up to the local shop and got her 10 cigarettes and when she came in, instead of sulking, I kissed her, apologised, and asked if she would like a drink. The storm had broken. Did we have sex then, later, or the following morning? Our most passionate sexual encounters often followed a big row.

Sunday evenings were special. There had always been a tradition of Sunday being the main meal of the week. Sometimes, if she was not gardening, she would cook dinner. She began to specialise in Eastern food, particularly Thai. There would always be a bottle of wine. When we sat down to eat, I would say a few words of thanks and appreciation, then we would begin. But there would often be an underlying tension, a realisation that the outside world was lurking in the background and its tentacles were taking hold of us.

Arron spent three years studying in Athlone, and there were times when the evening ended early as he had to be taken into town to catch the last bus. But there were other times when I would sense that Aileen was itching to leave the table, and I would hate her for the devotion she had to her work.

I would pour the wine and, after tasting and commenting on it, Aileen would hardly touch her glass. I knew then what was going to happen. I could not help myself. It was as if a death knell had been sounded. The weekend was over, she was moving away from me. After dinner, when we had tidied up, she would ask 'do you mind if I slip upstairs for a moment?' The bottle of wine would be half empty, her glass half full. I would fall into silence. I would ask about the film I had hired out to watch. I would go upstairs, often with the unfinished bottle. I would wait, and as it came closer to nine o'clock I would shout out that I was starting the film. I would wait in vain. When the film was over, I would lock up and go upstairs to bed.

I would not go into her study in the front room as that would be capitulation. I would sit up in bed waiting for her to come in. She was preparing for the next day, the next week, in college. I would be overwhelmed by jealousy, rage, sadness and loneliness. The emotions swirled around in me. I was slipping into hell. I wanted to love her, to hold on to and caress her. How could she be so thoughtless, so uncaring? Had she no idea what she was doing to me? Often it was after midnight when she came in. There would be silence. She would come to bed, reaching out for me, she would lean over and touch me gently and I would recoil and say nothing. And I would hate myself. And in the morning I would find it difficult to apologise.

17

It was strange, sitting in my chair, staring across at Aileen and thinking how I was going to organise her funeral. Where would we hold it? Who would say and do what? What music would we play? We had managed to construct a lovely ceremony for Luke, but now I was on my own. I looked at her and thought about asking had she any wishes, but realised that would be weird.

We were so used to sitting and planning, getting out the diaries, mapping out journeys and holidays. It was an intense pleasure. That Spring, Aileen spent hours plotting a journey across the north of Spain. We had been there a couple of times already, but we had never made it over as far as Santiago de Compostela. We would take the ferry to Santander and spend six nights staying in these paradors (boutique hotels). She had gone into each of their websites and she took delight in examining them, their rooms and menus, their proximity to the sea, and the travel time between them. She was full of excitement. And then the bomb went off, in the middle of an ordinary day.

I had been working in the study. It was early afternoon. She had come home early from work. It was a very busy time in the Institute where she worked. She had been complaining of a bad pain in her back before she had gone to work. She moved up the stairs slowly and painfully. I went around to her side of the bed and helped her sit down. I looked at her. She was distraught.

'My God, my love, you really are in pain.'

'No Tom, it's not just my back, I have breast cancer.'

Over the next three years the cocoon of love, in which I had been immersed for thirty-four years, came crumbling down. I had no idea what I was facing into. I had no idea what her words would come to mean.

The irony was that some weeks prior to this, Aileen had been worried about me. I had been feeling a bit weak: I was gasping for breath cycling up the mountain one morning and wondering why I had become so unfit. I thought I had the flu and stayed in bed. Suddenly I realised I was going to get sick, and went up to the bathroom where I vomited. My puke was dark red. I did not feel very nauseous and so thought, as I looked into the bowl of red fluid below, that it must have been the wine from the previous night. Then I realised that it was blood.

The doctor sent me to hospital. An endoscope could find nothing and I was told confidently that it was probably colitis. I was let out after a week when my haemoglobin had returned to normal.

That was some time in May. There was great excitement at home over the next month. Arron was finishing the final year of his degree in the same Institute where Aileen worked. Olwen was off down in the West of

Ireland at Irish college. Aileen was busy organising the end-of-year exhibition in which Arron was participating. She placed great emphasis on the exhibition. She saw it as an opportunity for the students to take pride in their work, for the Institute to show them off.

At the beginning of the month, she had become concerned about her breast. She went to the doctor who felt around and, while she was confident that there was nothing wrong, took the precaution of sending Aileen for a mammogram. During the X-rays, Aileen became concerned about the number of images they were taking. When they finally finished, she went into the room and demanded to see them. The radiographer refused vehemently. Aileen stood her ground and told them legally they had no right, she had not signed anything. So they relented and she saw the tell-tale white blobs just at the back of her nipple.

She had known the results of the mammogram on the Monday. She must have been devastated. I can only imagine her anxiety and fear, the sense of panic. She must have wanted to dissolve. The artistic issues that she had dealt with in her *House* work and *Deadheading* were imitating life. What had become stable again was now under attack. And, yet, for two days, she said nothing, to me or anyone. She decided to hold off until after Wednesday evening. Arron's results were out: he had received a First Class Honours, and she was determined to celebrate. I met her in town at the opening of an exhibition on American Art in the new extension to the National Gallery. We met up with Arron afterwards, and had dinner in Fitzers in Dawson Street. He had worked there the previous summer. I was in great form. It was a lovely summer evening. Earlier in the afternoon, Ireland had beaten Egypt 3-0, and qualified for the last sixteen of the football World Cup. I had walked into town. I was savouring the atmosphere as people came out of the pub into the early evening sunshine. Life seemed as good as it could get.

I noticed that Aileen was not as exuberant as usual. She did toast Arron, but I sensed there was something missing. I put it down to her bad back. I asked if her back was okay. She insisted she was fine. I suggested leaving the car in town: we could get a taxi home. I did not want her bad back interfering with the celebrations. I did not read the signs.

We had no idea how serious the cancer was. Two days later, I had an end-of-year department lunch. Aileen had been given an appointment with Oscar Traynor for a biopsy and so we decided that she would do this on the way to dropping me to the lunch. She was told it would only take a few minutes so I waited in the car. I was looking in the mirror for her to come out: she was late, what was taking so much time? I saw her walking towards the car. She was in floods of tears. She got into the car and said, 'He is going to remove my breast next Tuesday.' Having looked at the mammogram, Traynor realised that he needed to operate urgently. How or why did I go on to the lunch? How did I let her go back home on her own? But it was still early days. I didn't have a clue.

We had booked to go away for the weekend to Dungarvan in Waterford. We stopped off in Altmont Gardens on the way. It is one of the most beautiful gardens in the country. It was a beautiful day. We were shell-shocked. I was on the verge of tears all through the walk: every step down the path from the pond to the river was dripping with poignancy. To be in such a beautiful place in the middle of a nightmare. We made love that night. I kissed her breast goodbye.

After the operation we learnt that the cancer had spread to five of her lymph nodes. Even though it was diagnosed very early, because it had spread into the milk ducts it had moved very quickly. I learnt later from Traynor that he knew then that it was very unlikely Aileen would ever recover.

Aileen remained incredibly calm and focused during all this. She brought Arron and Olwen into her bedroom in the hospital and told them, then her mother and three sisters. Each individually, each in measured, reassuring tones. After her visit, Olwen asked me on the way home in the car if Aileen was going to die. I looked at her. 'Of course not,' I said.

I continued to cycle up the mountains all during June. I would call into Mount Carmel hospital in my cycling gear and timed my arrival to be there for breakfast. Aileen used to order the full Irish breakfast, but I ate most of it. Again, the sense of the two of us together, cheating and beating the system, and everyone knowing what was going on in that private bedroom but saying nothing. Were they being especially kind? Did they know that she was going to die, that her days were numbered?

And so we began a new journey, one which millions have made before us, and yet, like love itself, it is such an intense, personal experience that, no matter how much you hear and read about it, you never really get close to those feelings and emotions. We recognise and appreciate what it is to be in love, what it is to be in pain, what it is to die, but because they are essentially emotions we never share and understand them in the way we share thoughts and ideas. Over the next three years I watched Aileen die, and yet I have no real sense of what it is to die, what it was like for her. And yet I came close to death myself.

Aileen recovered quickly from the operation. They decided to delay the rigorous chemo regime until late August. We started going out and about. We booked to go the Gate theatre with Olwen and to eat before the show in the 101 in Talbot Street. It was a lovely sunny summer's evening. During the meal I began to feel a bit weak. I thought it was just the heat and I needed some air. I went downstairs to the street. Olwen came with me while Aileen got the bill. I stood on the street taking deep breaths and then collapsed in a heap. When I came round there were people all round. An ambulance was called. I was taken to the Mater hospital.

The woman who did the endoscopy had been told my history. Initially, she too could find nothing untoward. She was about to give up when she noticed something in the corner of my stomach. The CT scan revealed a large tumour in the lining. They took a biopsy, but it was going to take a day or so to get the results. I looked in the mirror in the bathroom the following morning and said to myself, 'You are a goner.' But I was so numb that it did not really sink in. Aileen was distraught. The following day I learnt that, effectively, I had won the cancer lottery. I had a very low grade maverick cancer – it was a stump tumour (a stromal tumour of unknown malignancy potential). They would have to remove it, and probably my stomach, but there was no immediate or substantial long-term threat.

I transferred to St Vincent's to be treated by Traynor, whom I had liked and who had an excellent reputation. I also liked the idea of us sharing the same surgeon. I recovered. Aileen did her chemo. It was a dreadful Autumn. The treatment of cancer has no respect for beauty. It ripped through her like a tornado, tossing off her breast and hair.

It was during this time that Aileen began to read voraciously about breast cancer, ordering books, scanning the internet, talking to women who had been on the same journey. She took to Jane Plant in a big way. The Plant argument seemed so simple. Why is the incidence of breast cancer in Asian countries miniscule compared to the West? The answer is that they do not have such a high dairy diet. Like many others, Aileen had grown up on a heavy diet of milk, butter and cheese.

Aileen embodied the belief. Plant was herself a scientist with a doctorate in biology. She amassed evidence to show that women who completely eliminated all dairy products from their diet were far more likely to survive. But research in the West consistently found no evidence that women who had high dairy diets were more likely to get breast cancer or, if they eliminated dairy products, were more likely to survive.

But when you are faced with death, it is good to have a regime based on firm belief. Aileen was an ardent practitioner and believer. Over the next two years, she never touched anything that had any dairy in it. She would meticulously question waiters in restaurants about the exact ingredients of each dish and the possibility of there being any dairy products in them. It was all a bit manic. She had been implanted with this huge fear that if a drop of dairy got into her system the cancer would explode again.

Aileen was determined that she would win, that she would beat the cancer. And, for a good while, it looked as if she would. She did the radiotherapy, took the drugs, and began exercising. She started to play golf. I got used to making love to a bald headed, one breasted woman. The crucial two-year marker began to loom. I put a bottle of champagne in the fridge – even though I knew Aileen would only ever have a sip. It was never opened.

Aileen had felt a pain in her back before that Christmas. She had a scan. She phoned me from the car park in the hospital. She was elated. 'There is no sign of any cancer.' But it turned out to be a false positive. They had not gone down the spine far enough with the scan. The pain spread to her side. Eventually she went back in for another scan. I had been down the country doing research. As I pulled into the house I noticed her car was parked at a funny angle. I knew it was a bad sign. I came into the kitchen. There was no smile. I could feel the fear running through me. I walked over to her. I just wanted to hug her. She stopped me and she said simply, 'There are some spots on my spine.' I burst out crying. What was this shit about there being some spots? It was as if she had told me she was only a tiny bit pregnant.

She looked at me and told me that she would still beat it, that she would be here to celebrate Olwen's 21st birthday. The following day she was back on the internet. She came into my study with sheaves of print-outs. 'It is a maximum of two years and it is very painful.' She got the last part right, but not the first part – she was dead within a year.

But she did not give up. She became even more determined. She went on sick leave. She heard from a friend who had been through breast cancer that there was a Dr Gonzalez who had trained in one of the top cancer hospitals in New York who was achieving remarkable results with his alternative treatment programme. She started following the programme immediately even though she did not get to see him until September. It was incredibly demanding. It was fortunate that I was on sabbatical and was able to look after her.

In those last months we retreated from the world, back into our cocoon. I brought her up her breakfast every morning. When she was finished, she would do the first enema, then I brought her up her first vegetable juice, then she had her bath. Afterwards she would work for a while – she continued working up to four days before she died. She was particularly involved in developing a programme which taught primary school children how to make their own films. In the evening there was another enema.

And on and on it went, every day, no matter where we were. She did enemas in the most amazing places. Even when she was back in hospital, I would have to bring in flasks of coffee and she would lie on the hard tiles letting the coffee drip up into her colon.

The good thing about the Gonzalez programme was that, although it was so much more demanding than the Plant regime, it did not bring a fear of toxic contamination. He did not go as rigorously with the dairy argument. He had her eating lamb's liver once a week. There were treats. I remember the excitement in her voice when she told me in November that Gonzalez had agreed that she could have a couple of slices of turkey for her Christmas dinner, but no ham.

During those final months, despite being in considerable pain, she did not miss an enema or treatment, drank her juices, and never failed to keep to her pill routine. She would get up at four in the morning and sit quietly at the side of the bed taking her 30 pills. Often, as she struggled from the bed, and hobbled out of the bedroom on her stick, I would ask, 'Are you okay?' and she would stop and say 'I'm fine my love.'

Trying to stay alive is damn hard work and took Aileen down many different paths. Besides following the Gonzalez treatment and seeing 'her team' in Vincent's (they did not get on very well with Gonzalez), she went regularly for reflexology. In her last weeks, by which stage the cancer had spread to her liver, she went to Paul Goldin, who was a well-known psychologist who specialised in hypnotherapy. She went to him because she was having great difficulty taking her 200 pills a day. He believed that it was a case of mind over matter. In fact her liver had swelled up and was pushing against her stomach. I thought Goldin was a bit of a chancer, but she was delighted with him. He made her tapes to relax. I used to drive her to him. I would wait for her. One time I caught a glimpse of her in the rear view mirror, hobbling back to the car and, as we headed off back home, she declared that not only was he going to get her to be able to take her pills, he was going to get rid of her pain and her cancer. I stared ahead with tears flowing down my cheeks.

18

And what of my own beliefs and practices during this time as I watched the love of my life slowly but surely dying in front of me? I was all over the place. Like Aileen, I grew up with God. He was a close friend for many years. I would love if he existed. Miracles can and do happen, but I have always thought that they were probably extraordinary cases of chance or mind over matter. Nevertheless, in those dark days as I walked around the local park in the early morning, I would scream out to God not to let her die. I hoped, but deep down I knew that there was as much chance of her not dying as her cut-off breast being restored.

God is hope. I live in hope that there is another meaning and explanation to all of this, to our joy and happiness, to our suffering and pain. I have no idea if there is life after death, or even what life after death means. I hope that we dissolve into a love supreme which is way beyond our imagination, which is way beyond human knowledge and understanding. But if God is infinite perhaps we should abandon thinking longitudinally and think laterally. He is by our side but we cannot comprehend him. Sometimes I think that trusting in God requires letting go all that we think is solid, material and real, even reason itself. It is a tall order to give up the air of certainty, mastery and control which we breathe so easily.

Whatever about God, during those fragile days I became completely entangled in magpies. They seem to have always been a part of my life. We grew up together. I was socialised into their logic. 'One for sorrow, two for joy.' It went on: 'three for a girl, four for a boy.' The rhyme goes on up: 'eight for heaven, nine for hell and ten for the devil's own self.' But in the folklore in which I was immersed, it was always whether there were one or two. I think it was my mother who first introduced me to them, telling me that it was a magpie who had stolen her ring. My uncle Bryan was obsessed with them. He told me that one day, in a desperate attempt to find a second magpie, he had driven his car into the ditch.

But magpies did not have any real significance in my life until Aileen got ill. Then, quite suddenly, they seemed to symbolically dominate me. In those dark days of deep despair, I was weak and vulnerable. I was desperate to see good omens.

Every morning when I went to see Aileen in Mount Carmel Hospital, there was a single magpie directly below her bedroom window. It was if he had been deliberately planted there. He stood cold, proud, majestic with a look of complete disdain and, when I shouted at him, he would casually hop around the grass, teasing me. It was as if he knew he was a bad omen and took delight in stalking me. All those mornings, afternoons and evenings while Aileen struggled to come to terms with her cancer, losing her breast, and the prospect of death, the magpie strutted its stuff on the lawn beneath her. The lord of the hop was already dancing on her grave.

Magpies are ferocious predators. I once saw a magpie take on a cat. It was walking along a very narrow wall and the magpie kept taunting the cat by blocking its path, squawking and flying away when the cat swept out at it with its paw. They are ruthless poachers. High up in the ivy at the back of the house I saw a magpie dive in on the nest of some blue tits. They cried out for help as the magpie ate their young. There was nothing I could do to save them.

But worse still, magpies prey on humans and their emotions. They are kill-joys. In those days, they seemed to know my vulnerability. They made sure to be alone when I was around. They teased me. They took delight in my sorrow.

The second I entered into the logic of the magpie I was lost. It seemed simple: one for sorrow, two for joy. But what happens when you don't see two immediately together in the same view? Can there be a gap between seeing the first and the second and, if so, how long can this gap be? Ten, twenty, thirty seconds sounds reasonable, but what about ten, twenty, thirty minutes? But then, if the time gap is that big, how do you know you haven't just seen the first magpie for a second time? Moreover, the rhyme says nothing about seeing. Does it count if you see one and hear another? And how long does the joy last? Minutes, hours, days, a lifetime? And what happens if you see one magpie and an hour later you see two. Does the recent sighting of the two cancel out the sorrow of the earlier one?

It seemed to me that single magpies were everywhere. In the hospital grounds, down by the river Dodder, and along the path into UCD. I slowly but surely became obsessed. I must have appeared slightly deranged, wandering around the park craning my neck around in circles, listening for their caw, looking up, down, back and around. And in between the sightings of solitary magpies, I would scream to the God I didn't believe existed and ask him what was he doing with the magpie, what was he doing to me, what was he doing to Aileen. I like the idea that all the time we think God is reasonable, that he is playing with us with magpies.

There is nothing in life quite like dying. Some years after Aileen died, when Arron, Olwen and I went to South Africa, we visited what is supposed to be the biggest bungee jump in the world. People leapt from the middle of this massive bridge and dropped 600 feet into the gorge below. But the biggest, most exhilarating, most challenging event in life is to leap into death. It is not something easily done. And although there is a lot to be learnt from looking on, as I did with the bungee jumpers, it is nothing like making the leap yourself. In those last five months, particularly after Christmas, Aileen stood at the edge of the abyss. She did not want to die. She grasped at straws, anything that would convince her that she was not falling into death.

She fought to the very end. Nevertheless, during those last months, there was a growing acceptance of her vulnerability. In February, she tried to begin a diary. She only kept it up for a few days. These are some of the entries:

11 February 2005

So, what the hell, let's get started. Mindlessness, a state of being. The goal through meditation and to de-clutter the mind, aid healing. And writing, another tool, but hardly mindless, surely mindful. Must be thoughts flowing through my mind that I can capture otherwise no activity. Yet I am happy a lot of the time to be fairly mindless, floating, daydreaming, or reading, lost in a novel, another story, a relief perhaps from my story.

15 February 2005

It's 12.45pm, a rush to get all my daily chores done. I took enzymes at 7.00am, finished about ten past and decided not to fall back asleep as I needed to take painkillers by 7.30. Decided to read the direction sheets for the pills Celebrex and Neurontin again to see how I could best safely increase the dosage. The pain in my spine has increased and hangs in all day like a persistent ache, until recently this was only happening erratically for a couple of days at a time then it would go. This has been with me now since last Thursday. Perhaps I grow impatient too quickly. It is now six days with me, it wears me down, I have to concentrate on being resilient, bearing with it, letting it be, waiting for it to pass. Hoping, praying that it will pass, that the pain will reduce. Meanwhile I try to increase medication to give me some further relief today.

The phone goes, Tom gets it downstairs. My love ever protecting me, shielding me, helping me, forcing me to look at my situation so I do not overdo things. He cancelled his birthday party this week. Made all the calls last night, it was to be small anyway, no family only pals we had not seen in a while. I could not argue, I have no energy or physical ability to make it happen. In that sense I really am an invalid. I can just about do enough to get by each day with little or no contribution to all the household chores.

One of my tasks had always been the laundry. Simple enough, taking the baskets of clothes down from the bedrooms to wash, dry and return to the bedroom ready for Mai to iron. It's rather sad and pathetic I think to see how I have to drag the basket of clothes down the three flights of stairs, I cannot carry the weight. Then I have to sit down on a stool to place them into the door of the washing machine. My arms cannot move at the angle required to place them into the machine, it gives me pain in my upper forearms, I had presumed this was referred nerve pain! I fill the machine this way. Sometimes having sat down and extracted the clean clothes in a similar manner I can manage to place them on the clothes horse to dry. Other days the bending to pick up the clothes one by one is too much for me. I like when I can still do my chores and when

I can find the ways around my physical impediments. I do feel sorry for myself at how pitiful this situation is. But that's all, that is the way it is and I know I must just get on with it.

My day, after taking the 7.30 painkillers, I continued to read and by 8.00am Tom came up with breakfast. Fresh orange juice, fresh organic fruit with fourteen grain cereal, nut milk, and yogurt, this all taken with the next dose of 30 mixed pills combining nutrients and enzymes. We read the paper together and by 8.30, Tom picks up the tray and moves on with his day. I stayed in bed and fell asleep again until 10.45. Then quick into action.

Down to make Juice 1, and eat 12 almonds and prepare coffee and enema bag. Then enema one which is completed by 12.30pm. Then next dose of enzymes. Then I have barely an hour to write. The day is still early, but the regime I am under is rigorous and relentless, I have to keep on the move and be conscious of time always so that I can comply with all the elements of the protocol with the order, and methodical application required. This is my job now and it is more demanding than any I have yet undertaken.

16 February 2005

What ails me today? Where am I? I have tears forming just beneath my eyelids, now they trickle down my face. Why? Feeling sorry for myself. I take a tissue, very soft and wipe the tears away. Am I recovered?

The pain has eased a little today I have dropped from a seven to a six on my chart. I don't know if it is because I have increased the pain medication to 15 Neurontin a day instead of 9, close to doubling the dose. The pain was intense and wearing me down, I had to take some action. I suspect it is only the painkillers giving me relief, not that the primary pain has receded. I will spend three days on this dose and then judge if I can reduce it.

Feeling sorry for myself. I feel trapped and so limited by what I can do. I weep again at my pain and restrictions. I am not sure if such weeping helps me release tensions or veers me to depression. Tom arrives back. It is 4.00pm. I am still in bed, although I have attended to all my duties and got myself lunch. I returned here as it is most restful on my back.

Thoughts flash across my mind, I love Tom, I grieve at the grief I see in him that I cannot comfort. I have been in so much pain over the past five days that I cannot make love. And yet I want to touch him so much and to be enveloped by him. Movement hurts, to roll from my back onto my side is done with so much labour to couch myself against the worst stabs of pain, that often despite being sore lying in the one position, I have to give up in my effort and resign myself to stay put. The great warmth and passion of his physical touch is a loss that I must hold off dwelling on, I must wait and hope this pain eases.

I am in such weepy mood today. Could it be the increase in medication or a wearing down of the spirit? Another bad day, no worse it's a low day. It's dry and grey outside and the light is beginning to fade. No wind or even breeze about only the dull sound of traffic and the sharper brighter sound of the birds singing sporadically. So many of them busy in the garden today, robins, blue tits, sparrows, blackbirds, thrush, and always the scavenger magpies.

18 February 2005

On my birthday, she wrote me the following poem:

> *Because I Love You*
> *Because I love you.*
> *I think on you and of you,*
> *And my eye roves over you*
> *this morning,*
> *and I long to feel and make love*
> *to your strong and tender being.*
>
> *And we did, and it was bliss,*
> *opening to you,*
> *my lover, my hero my wondrous man.*
> *That pleasure now even more precious*
> *because some days my body*
> *cannot come out of its pain and discomfort*
> *to bury itself in the joy of your move*
> *deep into me.*
>
> *Your Birthday,*
> *your day,*

my great pleasure to celebrate you.
Every pain and discomfort I have
seems to ripple through you also.
I don't wish that sweet love,
I adore your happiness and always wish
to be in the glow of that,
Like today.

I have such happiness in your being,
in your love
in loving you,
Happy Birthday Tom.

Despite her pain, she came out to lunch in Ranelagh that day, my last birthday with her. We were with Arron and Olwen. On the way back to the car, she stopped in the middle of Ranelagh. She was in pain, but she was smiling. I told her that I loved her. She looked at me and said, 'I know you do, it is just that I would love if you told me more often.'

The Sunday before Easter we went over to David and Deborah's for lunch. She was in good form. After lunch we sat in the living room. Quite suddenly, she complained of a crucifying new pain in her side. She could hardly move. She wanted to go home. I had drunk too much wine. I wanted to order a taxi, but she insisted on driving. When we got home, she spent most of the night awake. It was the first time I saw her crying with the pain.

Some time after Easter we discovered that the pain was the cancer entering her liver. She was sitting up in her bed in the hospital. She asked the matron if the results of the X-rays had come back. She said they had and that her consultant David Fennelly would be in the next morning to discuss the radiographer's report with her. Aileen said she wanted to see the report now. The matron refused. Aileen insisted. There was a phone call to David. Aileen got her way. The matron handed her the report. She took out her glasses. She read it and handed it over to me and, looking over her glasses at me, said, 'Well that's it.' The report was short and simple. 'Major disease deterioration with multiple new melanomas in the liver.'

19

I cry. Are they tears of self-pity? How can you cry for someone who has ceased to be, who no longer suffers pain and emotion? My tears are more for her when she was alive, that she had to leave so early, to leave a life of love and meaning, to leave the beauty of the world. I cry out but there is no response, just my voice, echoing in the stillness. I will never hear her voice again, her soft murmurings of love, her reassurances, her teases and cajoling. She would never talk to me again. I would never be able to share thoughts, ideas, feelings and emotions. I will never be able to see and understand myself, see through my petty frustrations and foibles, to pick through ordinary incidences of everyday life, the common as well as the strange and startling. I will miss picking over the bones of daily existence. Most of all, I miss that we never really got to talk about what it was like to die. If she had gone on a journey to the South Pole, I would have been full of questions. But since I didn't ask any questions about what it is like to die, I have no answers.

Was the desperate struggle to stay alive worth it? Would she have done it all again? What would she do differently? Would she have indulged herself more? What was it like to die without God, to die without believing that she would ever see me, Arron and Olwen again? I lie and think to myself, throwing words out into the abyss, waiting, hoping for the faintest of responses. All I have is my thoughts.

In the days and weeks after, I got up and performed my usual functions. I had no energy. I felt dazed and drained as if I was on some powerful drug. I wandered out into the world. I didn't feel part of it. I was amazed at how the world carried on as if nothing had happened. I wanted to stop people in the park, to scream at them: 'have you no idea what has happened?' It was the end of my world and nobody seemed to care. I wondered if I lay down on the path and cried would they pass me by. And if I told them that I had lost my wife, would they help me up, comfort and console me? Would they bring me home and put me back to bed? I tell myself no, we all have stories to tell, we all have crosses to bear, get over it, move on.

Was I stupid to have loved her so much, to have become so attached to her that I could not bear being without her? What was it that made me hold on to Aileen so tightly, so much so that when she died, I felt part of me had died? Wouldn't it have been easier if I had been less dependent and more detached? I would have been able to look at her, dead in the bed, and smile in the realisation that she was just another human being, that thousands of people die each minute, that in the scheme of things her life and death has about as much significance as a grain of sand on a beach.

Why could I not have laughed at how pathetic it all was? We become attached to people, animals, objects and we cannot let them go. Surely human beings should have evolved beyond this? It is really quite simple, the more attached you become to someone, the more you will feel the pain when you lose them. Is the trick not to become attached? Nonsense. It is through deep attachment to each other that we make love and create meaning. It is what makes us human. Death is brutal because life is so meaningful. We may be born and die as animals, but we live in meaning. We swim in a sea of love, attachments and meanings. We could not survive without them. We would be like fish out of water.

And the ordinariness of the world would take over. It was as if I was a forlorn infant, crying inconsolably in my cot and someone would come and dangle a sparkling band in front of me and I would become intrigued and distracted. The morning after she died, I was down as usual in the park with the dog, looking, walking and thinking about something mundane. Maybe it was only for a minute, maybe it was longer, going along as if nothing had happened, forgetting that she was at home in bed, dead. And it hit me, like an enormous wave, bowling me over. It was not just the thought of her. The thought came with a physical effect. I felt it in my stomach. It was as if someone had punched me. It is an intense pain.

I remembered that pain so well from when Luke died. I would be walking along, engaged in the ordinariness of everyday life, almost oblivious to my pain, and then the ice would crack and I would fall into this cold black abyss and I would wonder as I sank how I could ever have thought that the world would be normal again. This time I did not have Aileen to hold on to. Moreover, although I loved Luke dearly and felt his death enormously, I did not form the same bonds, the same intense intimacy. I did not realise myself through him the same way that I did through Aileen. When Aileen died I was lost.

I think I have become a bit addicted to being alone and lost. I like to disappear on my bike, often spending five or six hours lolloping around the Wicklow mountains. The beginning is always the same. I climb up the mountains behind Dublin, over the Feather Bed, down to Glencree and over upper Lough Bray to Sallygap, across the Military Road to the waterfall at Glenmacnass, and on down to Laragh. There I stop for a while, drink a coffee, eat a sandwich, consider the weather and ponder the rest of my route. I sit, look at clouds, sniff the air and wonder where I will head towards to get lost.

When I was young and out with Dad for a day's drive around Wicklow, I would see a turning and be full of curiosity as to where it went. I liked the excitement of travelling unknown roads, never knowing what was going to come up next. I would plead with Dad to go back and make the turning, but he never did. He was always emphatic that it went nowhere. Now I can and do take those turnings. Often, as Dad told me, they do lead nowhere and I have to turn back. Other times they bring me to the back of beyond and I am completely lost. Sometimes I stop and ask for directions, other times I keep cycling, turning corners, hoping I will come to a place I recognise, or a signpost that will put me on the right road. I may be lost for a while, but I know that I will find my way. I am safe. I have no fears of disappearing never to be seen or heard again.

The challenge of unknown roads is coming onto steep climbs. I am out of the saddle, pushing up and down on the pedals, wondering if the hill will ever end. Will it get steeper and steeper? Will I last to the top? I look ahead, there is no sign of relief. I try to think of the small pleasures that await me at home, a can of beer, a packet of crisps, a rugby match to watch. And, all of a sudden, the road levels and the climbing is over. Soon there is a downhill and I am coasting through rivers of white hawthorn, yellow gorse and red fuchsia.

I have become obsessed with losing things. I can spend hours going round the house searching for something small, like my glasses, my pen, my penknife, something which does not cost much, something which has no personal meaning, but I cannot give up the search. No matter how much I tell myself how ridiculous I am, there is this impulse to continue looking. I find myself rooting through clothes, drawers, chairs and couches. I stop and sit still and try to think when I had it last. Did I move it from its usual spot? Did I bring it anywhere? Maybe Olwen took it? I feel that if I give up, it will never be found. It is out there, somewhere. I am the only one who can find it. I am the only one who knows that it is lost.

I was out cycling across the Feather Bed with the Sugar Loaf in the distance, glistening in the early morning sun. I heard a small thud. I thought I may have lost my pump. I looked down. It was still there. I sailed on down the hill to Glencree. I looked down and saw my small bike computer had fallen off. I should have been able to let it go. I had had it since I first got the bike. It was always difficult to read. This was dangerous when once I was careering down a narrow mountain road and I spent too much time looking down to see what speed I was doing, and then I hit a pothole. I had promised myself to splash out and get a new one that had big figures. Here was an opportunity. I should have said to myself good riddance.

But it was all to no avail. Within seconds I had turned the bike round and was peddling back up the hill to where I thought I had heard the thud. But as I approached the spot I began to have doubts. Maybe it was further on up. To be sure, I backed up to the Feather Bed and walked back down the hill with my bike, carefully examining the grass verge, looking at stones, bits of paper, thinking that it will appear any second. I searched on, but it was getting late. If I kept this up I would be late for my rendezvous with Carol in Enniskerry. I gave it up, but only for the moment. Two days later I was back up searching the verge, this time more meticulously, with no time constraints. After half an hour, I gave up and cycled home. I thought about punishing myself for my loss by doing without a computer. I asked myself why I wanted to know the time, distance, average and fastest speed? I could do without one. Just because I lose something does not mean that I have to replace it, at least not immediately. I lost this battle with myself. The next day I got a new computer.

20

I cannot recall when the nightmares began. They came in waves of similarity with the odd tsunami thrown in. The first were the usual ones of loss. In one dream, I was in New York. I was going out partying. I locked my bicycle to a street sign. I partied late into the night. The next morning I woke up in bed and remembered my bike. I went back to the street where the party had been but I could not find it. So I borrowed my friend's bike and cycled back around looking for my own. I went into a store to get something, when I came back out my friend's bike was stolen.

Another time I was in some foreign city with Aileen. We were happy tourists, walking together down a busy street and something happened. People started running madly in the same direction, away from something awful. We tried to stop people to ask them what was happening, but nobody stopped. We began to run ourselves. The crowd was becoming thicker. We were frightened. I was holding Aileen's arm. I looked back to see if I could see what we were all running from and then I saw that Aileen had been dragged down the other side of a metal barrier. She tried to clamber over it, but she was dragged down. She got up. I eventually got over the barrier but she was gone. I got a glimpse of her head as she was dragged away by the crowd.

The worst in this series was when I wandered into a town. I have no idea where or when it was. It could have in the past or the future. The streets were deserted. I came to a large square. There was something going on. People were gathered at the far end. I could not make out what the attraction was. As I pushed my way up to the front, I saw a scaffold with five nooses. Everyone was silent. Then, from the far corner of the square, I saw these men lead out five women, all in white, all with hoods. They were led up onto the scaffold. They began to take off the hoods. The third woman was Aileen. Everyone was still silent. I didn't say anything.

Then there were dreams of being with her in various different places, at a party, shopping in a store, and being on holiday. I have this feeling of bliss, of being intensely happy. In one, I was in a hotel with her. We were walking down the stairs to the restaurant and, out of the blue, I realised that Aileen was sick, really sick. I stopped and looked into her eyes. She held my look as I asked if she was going to die. She smiled and said no.

In another, we were together somewhere, I don't know where, and we began to make love. It was luscious. I went to look into her eyes, but they were closed. I said something to her but there was no response. Then I realise that her body has become limp and finally that she is dead.

There were vicious twists in some of them. In one, and I don't remember if it was before or after that last one I described, we were talking away animatedly about buying a new bath and again I become frightened that she is sick and going to die. So I stop her talking and ask her if I am dreaming and she smiles and says no.

I did not fall into my grief for Aileen in the same way that I fell in love with her. It grew on me, slowly but surely. It enveloped my being. It was not that I had stopped loving. I still loved her passionately. It was just that she was dead. We had become so close over the years, so entwined. It was as if we were two trees that had grown up together, had become enmeshed, and then one died. I had nothing to hold on to. I could no longer hug her. I could no longer surrender myself to her. I could no longer make love to her. But I still loved her.

I am still learning to live without her. The pain is still enormous, even now, many years later. I am able to talk and think about her without that dreadful feeling in the pit of my stomach, without the tears welling up. I am now able to look at photos of her without being overwhelmed by the reality of what I have lost. I am able to write about her.

During the first couple of years, as with Luke, I spent most of my time going back over the last week of Aileen's life, trying to piece together those final moments. It was a way of trying to master and control the emotional experience. The more I thought and talked about the events of that week, the more I thought I would understand what happened. I could wrap her death up in language and, eventually, bury it, as I had her body.

This is what happens when I go to a funeral: I am burning with curiosity to know how the person died. I am substituting knowledge for emotion. I am trying to control death and the way it operates. As if somehow, in knowing exactly what had happened, the precise details of where, when and how the person had died, it would no longer be a mystery. I could explain it away.

But this is only partly what happened. I think in going back over and over those days I was not just letting go, I was also understanding what life is about. When I was growing up, I would spend hours in the local church doing the Stations of the Cross. I had been led to believe that in doing the stations I would understand, not just the suffering and death of Jesus, but the meaning of death, the meaning of my own life. I think that in going back over those closing days of Aileen's life, again and again, I was doing another form of stations. I was understanding my own life in terms of Aileen's suffering and death.

I did find enormous comfort and consolation in talking. I had learnt from Luke's death: the road to recovery is to talk and talk as much as possible with those who are willing and able to listen. There were so many people, family and friends, who listened to me going on and on about her suffering and death. In the first year I would meet her sister, Carol, a specialist in listening, and we would walk the dogs in the park in the early morning, often alone in the dark, in the depths of winter.

There was always a danger of my dying with Aileen. This is why mourning her became so important, devising ways of letting her go. I put large photos of her in the hall upstairs, inside the door downstairs and a smaller one in the kitchen. She is still a presence in the house. I have changed very little in the way the rooms are furnished and decorated. There are some things that I left completely alone, like her clothes. It took me five years to clear out her wardrobe. Is this a refusal to let go?

I know that if I hold on to Aileen too hard and too long, I am in danger of not developing new relationships. In the beginning I was fearful that I would not be able to love again. One of the days before she died, as I was sitting reading the paper with her after breakfast, she looked over at me and, once she had me looking in her eyes, she said, 'Tom, I want you be happy and I want you to be in love.'

Part of me did die with her. I am mourning the loss of who I was with her. When she died the identity and sense of self that I had developed with her also died. I have had to let it go. It is difficult to enter a deep, loving relationship because all that I really have come to know about myself was with, in and through her. When Arron was young I used to play swords with him. If I stabbed him, he would cry out and lie down and pretend to be dead. But then he would jump up and say 'new man out.' I am trying to do the same.

Like making love, while grieving is an intensely private, personal affair, it is also highly cultural. In the old days, in holy Catholic Ireland, there was an ability and encouragement to mourn in public. The dead were remembered at Mass on anniversaries. There was All Souls Day. There were Pattern Days when people went to tidy the graves. Women wore black dresses, men wore black armbands on their coats. In giving up the Catholic meaning of life and death into which I had been socialised, I had abandoned the traditional language and practices in which generations of Irish people had found comfort and consolation. But I had not replaced them with anything of my own. I was left again in no-man's land. I was struggling to create a new language, a new way of being and talking that is spiritual without being supernatural, that does not hide death, that tells the truth, that gives meaning and expression to what I am feeling, that provides some outlet and relief.

When Aileen died I went into another world. I was surrounded by family and friends, but I felt alone. As I began to move from the cocoon of my home into the wider world, I feared meeting other people. Social life is not only damn hard work, it can be impersonal, fast and furious. People work and play hard. There is little place or time for sentiment, particularly among strangers. The workplace can be treacherous.

Everyday life is full of uncontrollable encounters. I met neighbours, strangers, colleagues, and had to read and interpret them through what they said and did not say, what they did and did not do. I found many social encounters difficult to interpret. Were people frightened, confused, embarrassed, or simply uninterested? I felt as if I was being bombarded by a myriad of signs and words, trying to decipher their feelings and intentions. But it is often difficult to communicate feelings, particularly in organisational life.

I met a colleague early one morning. I was still weary and bleary. He was furious about something that had happened to him. He was pouring out venom. As his words splattered over me, I wondered what I could say and do to stop him, to calm him down, to remind him that the way organisations mistreat you is nothing compared to losing a loved one.

I am sure he too had lost someone dear and close to him. I am sure he too had grieved. But he was immersed in this minor issue. I had mixed feelings. I wanted to hit him and I wanted to hug him and tell him everything would be all right.

Maybe the problem was that he was so wrapped up in his own concerns that he did not see me. Maybe I had put on too brave a face and he could not see the huge melancholy that lurked behind my smiles. Or maybe he knew, but did not want to go there. He did not want death and loss to interfere with his life.

I wonder what he would have said if, instead of losing Aileen, I had had my arm amputated. Would he have been so easily able to ignore my loss? Grief is an invisible crucifix. Unless there is a physical sign of loss, it is easily forgotten, easily ignored.

The reality is that we do not want to deal with death and grief. We prefer to bury them deep within us and celebrate life and love. But we cannot have one without the other. We have thousands of books, stories, songs, poems, films and plays about love, but not so many about grief. It seems strange that we celebrate falling and being in love and yet those who have lost love, who are perhaps most in need of love, are given little public support or recognition. Death has become a deadly subject. Is there a way of making our mortality more central to our lives, of reminding each other about the frailty and beauty of life, of providing comfort and consolation to those who are dying and grieving without returning to the dark, fearful, repressive regimes of Catholic Ireland in which death was hung in almost every room? And yet, unless we hold death close, life will become more shallow and we may not be able to make love.

20

'Will I close the curtains?'

'No,' she said. 'I like the light.

I was fidgeting around, making excuses, like a schoolboy who could not start his homework. We had not made love for weeks and now, on the edge of death, she wanted to make love. How could she? How could I? Was this disgusting, some strange perversion? How could I have sex with a dying woman? How could I become aroused by an emaciated body on the verge of death? I was anxious and nervous. What if it was all too much for her? What if she died in the middle of making love?

Of course she had suggested sex before at strange times and in strange places, but this was very different. This was not about having sex. This was about making love. It was a celebration of all those wonderful times in the past. And so, in the blink of an eye in the eternity of time, I had moved from the first time, from lying on the floor in her sitting room, to the last time. I had never realised there would be a definite last time. I had never realised that it would become more etched in my mind than the first time.

Did she know this? Did she know what a beautiful memory she was creating? I think not. I think it was more about pure feeling, of being frightened, of wanting comfort and consolation knowing that she was no longer staring out the window into life but staring into death.

I did not have much time to think. It was all happening very quickly. I came round to her side of the bed. I looked into her face, into her eyes. She smiled. She was such a beautiful woman. I felt a warm glow. She could see that I was on the verge of tears and held out her hand and touched my face. She smiled again. She said nothing. There was nothing to say.

'How are we going to do this my love?' I asked.

'Will you help me on my side?'

I pulled back the sheet and put my right hand under her thighs and, with my left hand under her waist, tried to lift her towards me. The weight of her legs was enormous. I could not get enough leverage. She grimaced in pain. I was shaking with anxiety. Even if I did get her on her side, she was too close to the edge. I began to imagine the scene if she fell out of bed while we were making love.

It was time for patience. Her eyes were closed now. I paused. What was she thinking? I wanted to run out of the room, away from all this anguish, back into the past, back into those glorious mornings when we slipped easily between making love and eating, making love and drinking tea, reading, smoking, and making more love.

So many times in the past I had woken up hungry for her. She would be asleep and I would hold back from waking her. Then I would begin to slowly and gently run my fingertips up and down her body, as if they were a soft morning breeze caressing her. When she began to waken, I began to apply more pressure, moving from my fingertips to my hand. I loved to feel her breasts, to lick her shoulders and nuzzle into her neck. Sometimes I wondered if she was still asleep.

It is difficult to be alluring and erotic when you are emaciated. In the early months after she recovered from the chemotherapy and radiography, she struggled to look beautiful. She got herself a good wig and a prosthetic bra; to outsiders she still looked beautiful. The reality was that she was bald and breastless. It was sometimes quite shocking when I saw her naked. I would wince and look away as if I had seen something revolting. She would see me and, unable to hold back her emotions, would start to cry. My ghastly look was more devastating than the slash of any knife. Beauty is in the eye of the beholder, and I had denied her beauty.

I was so hurt by what was happening that I decided to get counselling. So I told a stranger about my feelings and emotions, about how difficult it was to see her breastless, about how I wanted to transcend these feelings of disgust, but that often they got the better of me. I seemed to be caught between wanting to have sex and to make love, a delicate balance between lust and love.

Aileen on the other hand seemed to become lustful and erotic. The closer she came to death, the more she wanted to be sexually alive. It was as if she could avoid death. She bought a couple of books on tantric sex and encouraged me to read them. The message was simple: stay in touch. Foreplay is not a means to an end. It is the end. It is about connecting physically, building up but delaying orgasm for hours. But I failed. I could understand the rationale. I could connect with the emotions, but I could not get into it.

In those days, she became skilled at the art of disguise and revelation. She would sit on top of me, wearing just her pyjama top. She would lean down and kiss me and then slowly sit back upright and begin to undo her buttons from the top down. As she got towards the end, she would pull the right hand side taught with her hand while slowly opening up and revealing her left breast.

Now it was the last time, the games of deception were over. I was crying. I lifted back the covers and, moving down to her legs, slowly inched down her bottoms. It seemed to take ages, she was not able to help, she could not lift her legs. It was like peeling paper from an ice pop. I could not see her. I could not read the expressions on her face.

What was she thinking as she felt me undress her for the last time? What was it like to begin to make love when you are beginning to die? On the verge of nothingness, looking into the abyss of time, was she trying to retreat into the cocoon of our love, a place of pure feeling and emotion, beyond language, just two bodies in space, holding on to each other for dear life?

It was as if she had found the secret of life. Love is not about what you say, it is what you do. It is going back to basics, back to touch as the source that generates feelings of happiness and belonging.

I had reached the end of the bed, her pyjamas were off. I crawled back behind her.

'Are you all right my love?'

'I'm fine.'

I began to caress her. I felt myself caught between life and death. I had no idea what was going to happen next. The idea of becoming aroused seemed as likely as a tiny balloon reaching the moon. And yet I felt a responsibility. I was not alone. She was not alone in all this death and dying. I was alive and I had the gift of life. In the midst of Aileen falling into nothingness, I could remind her through touch and feeling of the beauty of making love.

I stroked and caressed her and reached in under her arm to hold her breast. As I kissed the back of her neck, I was amazed how easily I was aroused. I was not elsewhere, I was with my love. The feel of her soft skin, the scent of her perfume, her gentle response to my movements, and the determination to fulfil her desire, to give her pleasure, made the moment serene.

There was something beautiful, timeless and ironic about it all, exploding into life while she was dying. We create meaning in that small gap between life and death. In the history of time, we are little more than mayflies, born to die the day we are born. In having sex, we take pleasure, we reproduce, we continue life from one generation to the next into infinity. When we make love we dissolve into a meaning that goes beyond time.

21

Postscript

(Aileen, December 2004)

Woof and meow were among the first snatched words they exchanged dancing close on a crowded dance floor, an attraction and excitement in them to have met just as the dance was nearly over. She liked his voice, its depth and resonance, his physical shape and the wideness of his smile. She has always felt that she fitted into his arms so perfectly, her head rests at just the right height into the nook of his chest beneath his shoulder and even on that first night, it felt good. There was an immediate sexual arousal. Her best friend described the 'electricity' she felt passing between us when in later months we both met him by accident strolling down Grafton Street.

Over that first weekend she met him she learnt how funny, witty, and smart he was but also how bold and irreverent. Attentive, with a softness and vulnerability that was deep in him, that she could feel long before he could express it. The expression of that enormous ability to love surfaced slowly over the years, usually released when much drink was taken. He didn't talk often of his love for her in those early years but when he did, it was so powerful, moving and intense that she could carry the glow of it within her for months. It was as though he had to measure how often he expressed his love for her or it would be belittled, become a rote formula, a meaningless babble of words.

He was intellectually challenging, inquisitive, probing and honest. She admired him. He had echoes of the wisdom and constancy of her father, without the gung ho positivism; he seemed to hold a calmer, deeper oneness with life. But wisdom, kindness and compassion are often the outcome of a deep emotional pain. Pain that is hard to set aside, to recover from, that is absorbed into the essence of being. Life moves on and peace, contentment even happiness can coexist with that imbibed presence of pain. It settles below the surface, prompted at times by sparked memories, emerging unbidden.

She let him go for a while. Following the dance they spent all the time they could in each other's company. She felt full of loss when she waved him off from the pier as he took the boat to return to France after that brief weekend. They wrote immediately, long letters, exploring each other, revealing the self. But she got distracted, after time he drifted into her past. When he came home many months later, he phoned her, she was embarrassed, did not want to talk to him. She asked her sister to say she was out. She stubbornly refused, with all the maturity of her twelve years; she knew it was mean and dishonourable of her, insisted that she talk with him. Her sister's memory was more intense than hers of the romance she had witnessed as she had waited longingly for his letters to arrive in the past. Angry with her she took the phone, and then she heard his voice. She fell straight into his arms again from that moment.

All the qualities she grew to love and admire would have passed her by if there had not been that initial animal attraction, if he had then not been able to satisfy her awakening sexual desires. He did that and she married him at twenty, content for however long it would last but with little faith in the 'for life' clause. She had no idea what a hugely loving, intense and fulfilling relationship would develop in the decades that have since passed.

When they first danced she was sixteen and he was eighteen. He was on a brief weekend home from France for Easter. He was working teaching English in a wealthy boys secondary school. He 'ran away' from home initially to Spain where he ended up living in a monastery and was then through the good offices of the monks placed as an English tutor with a kind Spanish family. It was not the type of emancipation from his childhood that he had been seeking but it helped settle him and gave him time to be 'alone'. His spirit roused her. At sixteen she was living in a loving family with all of its own complications, and felt caged and stifled. She longed for 'freedom' for her life to get under way. She had the habit on the worst days of pent up frustration of skipping school and taking the bus to airport to watch the planes take off or of going to the port to watch the boats heading out into her undiscovered world.

This man is still the love of my life, he has brought me huge and immense love in our passing through time together. We were so young when we met that we grew up together, faced into a life together, that brought joys and the sorrows our way. We had three beautiful children, our youngest son died in an accident at home when he was ten months old. It reinforced our love for each other and for our other children. We have been of great strength to one another and have understood since our young son's death just how fragile and unpredictable life is.

When I got cancer he was distraught, I asked him would he tell me more often that he loved me. It became easier and harder. With huge emotional honesty, care and passion he loves me and asks constantly 'do you know how much I love you?' And I know, see and feel his love now, all the time. His parents never hugged him. His mother believed children should be hardened against being too emotional. She believed it made one too dependent on other people. She was in a difficult marriage for many years when his father was an alcoholic. The father, while an affectionate man, had difficulty showing it and was the product of a troubled upbringing himself. Hence his son at seventeen ran off to Spain, full of a fighting spirit to escape his childhood and survive in the world independently.

We cannot survive well without love. My man loved me hugely from our earliest days together. But I didn't feel wholly secure in that love until he learnt to speak of his love for me freely as the emotion arose, until he forgot about measuring it so it would be more profound in the occasional telling. Since he gave in to his love and emotion for me, not only do I exist in the knowledge of his love but I float every day in the pleasure and joy of my man's exquisite expression of it.